"A very touching story that poignantly illustrates that while none of us have discovered 'the truth,' the spiritual reality is far greater than we have been led to believe."

—*New Age Journal*

"Sheri serves the world well by revealing her intimate and successful travels down the road of non-traditional healing."

—Walter Beebe, President, New York Open Center

"I could not stop reading this profoundly simple account of personal transformation and healing. An inspiration!"

—Barbara Marx Hubbard, co-founder, Global Family

"An extraordinary personal testament of experiencing the basic alchemy of creation."

—Hazel Henderson, author of *The Politics of the Solar Age*

Combining such simple concepts as self-love, acceptance, and forgiveness with visualization techniques, characterized breathing, and meditation, Sheri Perl has developed an extraordinary program for spiritual and physical health. So read on—achieve greater peace of mind, find your deeper self, and begin healing your body and your mind.

HEALING FROM THE INSIDE OUT

HEALING FROM THE INSIDE OUT

Sheri Perl

A SIGNET BOOK

NEW AMERICAN LIBRARY

PUBLISHER'S NOTE

The ideas, procedures, and suggestions contained in this book are not intended as a substitute for consulting with your physician. All matters regarding your health require medical supervision.

SIGNET TRADEMARK REG. U.S. PAT. OFF. AND FOREIGN COUNTRIES
REGISTERED TRADEMARK—MARCA REGISTRADA
HECHO EN DRESDEN, TN, U.S.A.

SIGNET, SIGNET CLASSIC, MENTOR, ONYX, PLUME, MERIDIAN and NAL BOOKS are published by NAL PENGUIN INC., 1633 Broadway, New York, New York 10019

First Printing, January, 1989

1 2 3 4 5 6 7 8 9

PRINTED IN THE UNITED STATES OF AMERICA

To my mother, in deep appreciation for the love and trust that supports my life.

Acknowledgments

There is no question in my mind that this book had to be dedicated to my mother for service above and beyond the call of motherhood. She has never failed to be a source of support and love, the quality of which is deeply nourishing. I therefore acknowledge her again, and say, as I have said to her many times before, "thank you."

Although I have dedicated this book to my mother alone, I am grateful that a section for acknowledgments exists as there are so many others whose names merit mention. Beginning with those family members and close friends who served me during the time of my illness, I would like to offer my sincere appreciation.

To my sister, Sondra Perl, who literally stood by my side and held my hand while I underwent the most difficult experiences of my life, I am deeply indebted. Now, as then, Sondra is an integral part of my life. I am happy to say that we are presently able to share the joyous aspects of existence. Sondra, by the way, is happily married, has three children, and recently published her own book, *Through Teachers' Eyes.*

I would like to thank my brother Richard Perl for his support and love. Although he was only a child during the years of my illness, his love and concern were apparent to me. A graduate of Columbia Law and Business School, he is also deeply involved in healing and spiritualism. He is, and I'm sure always will be, supportive of my work and my life.

Robert Perl, my youngest sibling, was too young to be actively involved in the crises that came with my illness. His love and concern, however, were always a part of my life. Today he shares my deep interest in healing. He is a constant source of encouragement where my work is concerned and in my life.

To our father, Herman Perl, I owe much gratitude. He, with his strength, power, and enthusiasm for life, taught me at a very early age not to give up or give in too easily. He instilled in me a zest for living life to its fullest, and when this was not possible, he taught me to work toward it anyway. He stood by me throughout the trying years of my illness, encouraging me and fighting with me the enormous battles that were in my path. There are no words to express how much I love him. Although he is not physically present on the earth today, it is my belief that his spirit exists and is aware of mine. I feel that he is proud of this book. As I look at the sculpture sitting on my desk of a young girl clutching her abdomen in pain, a piece of art that my father made in my image, I know that his energy is indeed a part of this book.

I would like to mention my late grandparents, John and Irene Oxfeld. My life and well-being were always a matter of great importance to them. Their memory is held dearly in my heart. Many thanks, too, to my uncle Bernie Oxfeld, whose assistance and concern were always available to me at any time throughout my illness.

I want to acknowledge my ex-husband, who saw me through the most difficult years of illness and tender years of adjustment.

To those medical people who served me and fought for my life I am also deeply indebted.

Although I have been asked to conceal his name, I must thank the wonderful man and doctor without whose skilled hands and brilliant mind I might not be here today. I hope, my dear one, as you read this that you know who you are. Know also that you have my love and appreciation always.

Dr. Barry Mankowitz, the brilliant young surgeon whose personal care and attention assured my existence, served me above and beyond the call of doctorhood. I will never forget what you have done for me, Barry. Thank you.

I would like to thank Ruth Kale, my very excellent postsurgical nurse, who helped me to adjust to and handle my ileostomy as well as to recover from the depths of severe illness. I would at this point like to acknowledge all nurses for the enormous role they play in the healing process of the patient. Especially when a patient first begins the long climb back to health, nurses play a vital role. This can be a tiring process in which both nurse and patient are tried to their fullest capacities. I have been very impressed by the devotion and dedication of nurses. They work with patients on a daily basis while the patients are undergoing the most difficult ordeals of their lives. As one patient recovers, the nurses move on to other cases.

Another wonderful nurse who assisted me in my recovery from surgery is Barbara De Wall. Patient and supportive, Barbara was always a welcome sight in my hospital room.

To the spiritual healer whose power and energy worked to reverse critical illness in my body at a time when my medical doctors felt powerless to effect a change, I offer unending gratitude. The late Harry Edwards, healer, teacher, writer, and friend, was a force in my life that served to heal me and to open the doors to my study of spiritualism. Once those doors were open and years of study ensued, I was fortunate to discover and become closely acquainted with Jane Roberts and Seth, the two finest teachers of psychic phenomena that, in my opinion, ever existed. To them I offer my love and gratitude for the tools necessary to understand myself and my personal power.

To those who serve me presently in my life I would like to offer my gratitude.

Dr. Daniel Present, my current physician, makes going to the doctor a pleasant experience. It was he who encouraged me to have reconnective surgery five years ago and for that I am deeply appreciative. To Dr. Irwin Gelernt, who performed that surgery brilliantly, I offer my heartfelt thanks.

Much thanks to my editor, Matthew Sartwell. Sharing my vision for this book from the start, he has encouraged me to write it in accordance with that vision.

I want to express my appreciation to Anne Marie O'Farrell. My dear friend and agent, your encouragement and support have always helped me to stay on course. Thank you.

For the lives of my wonderful sons Aaron and Daniel, who add immeasurably to my life and sense of purpose, I am most grateful. You boys may be too young right now to understand how happy you have made me. However, as you grow older, you may read this. Therefore I want you to know that I love you, and that I am very proud of you both. Wherever you may travel, whatever course your lives may take, know that I will always be there for you in love and devotion.

I have saved the last thank you for my husband, Jerry Migdol, whose existence and presence in my life has given me the peace and serenity, strength and security to sit tucked away in my study every day and compose this book. Although most people who relate to Jerry in his real estate business may not see the inner spirit that propels him, he is as acutely aware of the concepts in this book as I am. He lives his life out of that knowledge. It is always he who is the first to point out the necessity of trust when the chips are down, and to him this is not just a load of concepts. He lives his life from a center of trust, hard work, and as he puts it, "hard play." Through his words and his example, I have grown to be more trusting and more playful, and our life together is richly woven with threads of love and appreciation. To you, my darling, I offer all my love and gratitude for your unshakable strength and support, your nourishing love and warmth, and for the most wonderful decade of my life.

Introduction

I have written this book to honestly share a portion of my life experience with you. This experience, of being very ill and fighting for survival, took me down many different roads and eventually led me to open the doors to psychic exploration. Once they were open, I was the recipient of a most miraculous healing. In a sense writing this book is one way of expressing my gratitude for the life that I am presently leading, and for the knowledge that I have been so fortunate to gain.

It is my sincere hope that this book will inspire as well as guide each of you into a greater understanding of yourself, of the spirit realms, and of your own enormous potential for health and happiness.

Each day that I live I am more fully convinced that the ideas presented in this book have a real and practical basis in reality. It becomes all the more clear, when the stress level in my life rises, that it is the understanding and application of these ideas that maintain my health and sense of balance.

Because I have journeyed so far to rest on the calm shores where I find myself now, I am acutely aware of how it feels to be on the rocky seas. It is therefore my privilege and pleasure to pass on whatever knowledge I have gained to you. If it serves and guides you, then my wish will be fulfilled.

Part I

-1-

An Overview

As I look back at my past, it is hard for me to believe that I, as such a young woman, could have suffered and triumphed over so much pain and illness. As a mother of two I can't imagine how I could ever endure watching my sons suffer as my mother stood by and watched me. And yet sitting here now, I have no regrets. I know that in an odd and yet very real way, I am somehow better, stronger, wiser, and more compassionate as a result of what I have been through. Not that I recommend learning through suffering. If I have my way, throughout the remainder of my life, I hope to learn my lessons from joyous experience. However, most people do not stop to question the course they are on unless they run into difficulty. Unfortunately, in our society, suffering gives way to pondering, while positive experience is simply enjoyed. This was certainly true for me until events in my life led me to search for help and answers in realms that at one time I would have considered unfathomable.

I first became ill at the age of sixteen with ileitis, a chronic disease that attacks the ileum, or small intestine. While I underwent two years of medical treatment, the disease progressed into my colon. The spring of 1969 found me fighting for my life on an operating table. Thanks to the skilled hands of two very wonderful surgeons and my strong will to live, I managed to recover from the depths of severe illness.

My next challenge was to accept and learn to live with the result of my second surgery: an ileostomy. Although the

United Ostomy Association, Inc., in California estimates that there are 1,500,000 ostomates in North America today, when I woke up to discover that I had to wear an appliance on my body for the collection of waste materials, I felt alone and humiliated.

The adjustment to life with an ileostomy was not an easy one for me, and I looked forward to a time when I would return to surgery to terminate it. However, a second illness interrupted my plans. Chronic hepatitis, which was considered medically incurable at the time, was diagnosed a year and a half later, after extreme weakness led me to return to my doctor for tests. When I finally understood that there was no sure answer to my ills through traditional medicine, and knowing all too well how devastating illness can be, I contacted British healer Harry Edwards purely out of desperation. To my amazement a most incredible healing took place, a healing so thorough and complete that it spurred me to open the doors into the entire realm of psychic exploration. As the details of that healing are revealed in this book, I hope that they will have a similar effect on you. As you will see, the unique way in which the events unfold illustrates clearly, at least to my mind, the existence of an unseen world, a world of spirit, a world beyond and yet within this very one of which we are a part.

This concept seemed nearly unbelievable to me twenty years ago, although by now it has been incorporated into the very fiber of my existence. I do not ask that this be true for you, although I'm sure for some of you it is. For those of you who find spiritual healing hard to accept, I ask only that you keep an open mind as you interpret the events surrounding my recovery. I believe that you will find yourselves as I was, amazed, curious, and overwhelmed. At the very least, I hope that you will begin to question the nature of reality and respect the power of your thoughts.

I hope to show in this book that the nature of reality is not merely physical and that thoughts are not only mental. And that we, as individuals, have far more power over our lives than we have ever conceived. I also hope to show that we are not alone in an uncaring, unfeeling universe, creating our individual existences, but are instead surrounded by friends, visible and invisible, whose energy and love can most assuredly assist us.

With that in mind, the last sections of this book will delve into the many different methods that can and should be used if you are interested in learning how to use your mind to tap into your own power and the greater power of the universe. The methods of personal healing described in this book are those that I have used and still use today. I hope that you will eventually develop a daily practice in which time is put aside to explore these different techniques, for the psyche is like a muscle; it needs attention if it is going to grow.

The truth is that many of us are unaware of what we are thinking and not clued in to the pictures that we are forming in our minds. We are often greatly shocked when things do not turn out as we would have liked them to, and blame God or circumstance. It is my contention that taking the time to look inward (the exercises given in this book will help you to do this) is all that is needed to begin making the connections between our thoughts and the experiences that seem to have been thrust upon us. Once those connections are made, we can start changing the thoughts and suggestions that we are feeding ourselves. That in itself can have the most marvelous effect on our lives; so much so that if this book were about thinking alone it would be a powerful treatise indeed. However, this book is also about the existence of an inner, unseen world of spirit that I believe exists within our physical one. It is about the inner, possibly unseen, but certainly never unfelt portion of yourself that is your spirit and the source of your energy.

You can learn to harness and use that energy to bring about what you need in your life. HEALING, in capital letters, means putting into your life something that is needed or longed for, whether it be satisfying work or a nurturing love relationship. Healing from the inside out means going inside to the spiritual source of your power, healing first from the psychic, spiritual, feeling-thought plane, and then experiencing the change as the energy filters out into the physical layers of your body and your experience. This does not exclude the use of medicine or of any technological advancement that helps you. However, it does most assuredly include working with the contents of your own mind and opening yourself up to new possibilities. It's easy to take a Tylenol when you have a headache and push all this psychic stuff aside, because most likely the headache is going to go away anyway and you don't have to worry. But heaven help you if you come up with a so-called incurable disease, as I did, and you're unwilling to explore the inner psychic content of your being or your universe. In my opinion, you're in for a hell of a lousy time as you struggle with pain and suffering, confusion and despair.

Twenty-two years after I first fell ill, I am writing this book. I have been teaching these concepts for ten years. However, the requests of many of my students and my own inner urgings have led me to reach out still further and write my story in depth. In this way I can share what I have learned in the hope of paving the way for another. Putting up signposts along the road that say, "I have been here. It is safe to try. It is not foolhardy to believe. It is not unrealistic to dream!"

Because I have been so fortunate as to find my way back to health, joy, and a full life, I want to spread that joy outward. However, my use of the word *fortunate* should not fool you into thinking that the joyous aspects of my life are the result of luck. I have worked with psychic healers, medical healers, and above all with my own conscious mind to bring about the changes that are mine. This is not beyond any of you. All of you possess the ability to create physical health, mental health, and a joyous fulfilling life. I hope through this book to show you many of the ways this can be done. However, the strongest message that I wish to impart is that you are the doer, and that the keys to change rest in your willingness to turn them. I hope to demonstrate to you that even difficult situations are not necessarily hopeless, and that by turning the keys on the inside, the picture on the outside can change dramatically. It did for me. Therefore, in gratitude I want to share all that I can with you in the hope that my experience will serve as a torchlight to help illuminate your path.

- 2 -

My First Illness

In the summer of 1967, I was touring the West Coast with a group of thirty girls when the first symptoms of illness appeared. The daughter of a wealthy businessman, I was a healthy, attractive, normal sixteen-year-old girl. I was in no way prepared for the events that were about to take place in my life.

The teen tour had started off on a high note. I had become close with eleven other girls and we instantly formed a clique. We called ourselves "the dirty dozen," passed around pictures of our boyfriends, compared and tried on each other's clothing, and engaged in the normal conversations of young women. There was nothing that could have prepared me for the severe pain that seemed to come upon me from out of nowhere one morning while we were visiting the Grand Canyon. While all the other girls were getting dressed to go down to breakfast, I found that I was unable to get out of my bed. "I must have eaten something," I thought, "this will pass soon." I had never experienced serious illness before. Naturally, I assumed that the sharp abdominal pain would go away as mysteriously as it came.

I informed my mother of the difficulty I was having two days after it began. The sympathy in her voice made me feel like bursting into tears, and yet I fought hard to hold my emotions inside. I wanted so to be grown up. Determined not to appear the baby, I refused my mother's requests to return home, visiting more bathrooms in Disneyland than exhibits.

The rest of the tour was a nightmare. From the time the symptoms began until our arrival back in Kennedy Airport eight weeks later, there was not one day in which I wasn't plagued with severe discomfort. I became increasingly crankier and more preoccupied as my illness progressed. As a result, the other girls, who considered themselves very worldly and sophisticated, grew impatient. I felt very shut off from them, even disliked. I ached with loneliness.

During the tour I grew used to the condition, which somehow made it more bearable. I could pretty much expect to have cramps periodically throughout the day and an intense case of the runs every morning. But frighteningly, a new symptom developed the last ten days of the trip which was much more acute and disturbing. I began to experience pain in my esophagus whenever I swallowed. Simultaneously, I felt an itch behind my right ear. I knew that I wasn't going crazy, but all of this was very unnerving. Because the other girls seemed so annoyed with my complaints, I was afraid to open up to them. Therefore, I held my fear inside of myself, along with the hope that when I returned home I would see a good doctor capable of curing me.

I could clearly see the concern on both my parents' faces when we finally met again at Kennedy Airport. They, too, had expected my condition to clear up by now, and they were anxious for me to start medical treatment. My mother watched me in amazement as I cried and kissed each girl good-bye, promising to write and pretending a kinship I didn't feel. She knew that I felt estranged from the girls, and was surprised to see the measures I would take to pretend otherwise. I was a little surprised myself, but while I remained in the company of others, I felt the pressure to fit in. I was relieved now to be separate from the girls and the traveling. No longer would I have to contend with filthy train bathrooms or the impatient looks of annoyance from the other girls. The sight of my father in the front seat, dark and handsome, like a sheik, and my mother, blond and fair-skinned, like an angel, each so strong and in their own way, physically beautiful, created a feeling of security. I couldn't remember a time in my entire sixteen years when a problem arose that they could not solve. Yet a sense of foreboding pervaded the air as we drove to suburban New Jersey.

My parents were determined that I see a doctor immediately. Of course, I knew that this was inevitable, and I feared it greatly. I presume that most people don't particularly enjoy going to the doctor, but to me it had always been an enormous trauma. I received more than one polio shot on the sidewalk outside my doctor's office, when the nurse had finally put a stop to my getaway. I found taking my clothes off and sitting on the white paper uncomfortable and embarrassing. The very thought of needles scared the hell out of me. It is a good thing that I had no idea of what lay ahead.

As the car pulled into the circular driveway that led to our home, I felt as if I had never left. Everything looked just as it had before, green and lush and beautiful. My brothers Rich and Bob were home to greet me, along with "Dee" —Louise Miller, our live-in governess. She had joined the family at Richard's birth in 1957. Our cook Mamie, who made the best southern fried chicken in the world (as far as we were concerned) had prepared her specialty in honor of my return. Everything was just as it had been, except for one thing. I was unable to eat my chicken dinner without experiencing the familiar pain in my abdomen, and the unfamiliar pain and itch combo in my esophagus and ear.

An internist, a friend of my father's, was the first doctor to see me. He had been treating my father for high blood pressure for a few years, and my parents thought that he might be able to help me. At least they knew him. Surely it would be a good place to start.

On the day of our appointment I was as nervous as a jackrabbit. I thoroughly resented the experience from start to finish. My mother and I sat nervously together in the waiting room for quite some time until a nurse took my personal history and then led me to a room where I was instructed to undress and put on one of those obscene paper gowns. I was then asked to trot off to the bathroom and provide a little urine sample, and then to come back and sit on the table and wait for the doctor—how I hated that white paper! When the doctor entered the room, I was glad that he was a small man and not very intimidating. Nonetheless my stomach seemed to turn over a few times as he examined me, drew blood from my arm, and then ran some X rays of my esophagus. Due to my obsession with the esophagus problem, I completely glossed over the abdominal pain in my discussion with the doctor, which led him to diagnose and treat only the esophagus situation. He said my esophagus looked a little swollen in one place, that it was probably a result of nerves, and he prescribed a muscle relaxer to be taken a half hour before meals. He said that it would probably improve within a week or two and that he didn't find anything else wrong with me.

My mother and I left. As I look back I realize that this day marked the beginning of our medical companionship. As we drove to the pharmacy to fill the prescription, I was satisfied. The dreaded doctor's appointment was over and I was free again to live my life. My mother, on the other hand, expressed her dismay over the fact that no light had been shed on my digestive problems. She wanted me to see another doctor, while I just wanted to be left alone. I had accepted the stomach problem. I didn't want to see it get in the way of my enjoyment any more than it already had. My boyfriend was about to leave for his freshman year in college, and we wanted to attend a number of social events. I was anticipating an eventful and exciting junior year as a member of the Millburn High School cheerleading squad, a status that I had worked very hard to achieve. I didn't have time to be sick. Moreover, I had grown so used to the symptoms that I figured the best action was to take no action at all. Of course, my reasoning was powered by my fear of doctors. My parents were aware of this, and were not going to go along with it. They had enormous faith in the medical profession and felt that once we found the right doctor, my problems would be over. The decision was handed down to me by my father while he sat in his chair at the head of the long dining-room table: I'd see another doctor and we would not give up until I was completely well again. It was inconceivable and ludicrous to my parents that this should not come about. They could not accept the notion that I would just continue to live with pain and discomfort. My father's presence was always very strong and I knew that I could not buck him. An appointment was made.

The next man who treated me was a gastroenterologist, a specialist in digestive disorders. Dr. Marvin, with whom I would eventually have a long and involved relationship, seemed very alien and distant to me as he first walked into the examining room. There I was, biting my nails, wearing one of those daring little examining robes, sitting on the white paper. My mother stood just a few feet away from me. I sensed a ripple of fear shoot through both of us as our hope walked through the door.

The doctor was not very cheerful or communicative as he went about his business of listening to my heart, taking my blood pressure, and pressing on my stomach to see where it hurt. My mother held my hand as the doctor drew blood from my other arm. No one knew better than she how terrified I'd always been of needles. Holding hands became a ritual with us, symbolizing to me that we were both in this together. The doctor then asked me to drink two large glasses of a pink chalky liquid and explained to me how the barium would illuminate my intestinal tract, thus allowing him to have a closer look inside. As I lay on the cold X-ray table with a cup in my hand and a straw in my mouth, Dr. Marvin, from inside a booth, would say, "Now take a drink, drink, drink, now hold it, hold your breath, hold it, okay, breathe."

My mother and I couldn't believe it when the doctor reported that the X rays showed nothing conclusive. There was no diagnosis to be made and no treatment to be instituted. He recommended trying antacids but no further instructions were given.

My mother was thoroughly disheartened. I was so glad to get my ass off the white paper and onto the seat of the car that all I could experience was enormous relief. As we drove home, I resolved to sweep the symptoms under the rug whenever I could. My plan was to find a way to just live around them.

I continued this way throughout the rest of the summer of 1967 and into the fall. We were now approaching 1968, a new year. I was moving toward it with a condition that was bearable, yet constant. I made certain adjustments in order to deal with my symptoms. For example, by this time I had developed such a bad case of hemorrhoids that immediately after stepping out of bed in the morning, I would start running a bath. This way I could dive into the warm soothing water as soon as my angry bowels granted me parole from the toilet. Beyond such small adjustments, I tried to maintain what I considered to be a normal existence, attending school and interacting socially. As a teen I did not understand my fear or my motivations. I constantly pushed myself to keep active, and cover up my illness rather than address it.

My home life was bustling and active. My younger brothers, ten-year-old Richie and eight-year-old Bobby, were not fully aware of my illness. My parents didn't believe in telling children upsetting things. For the most part I behaved normally, and an occasional whine was not seen as anything out of the ordinary. Sondra, my older sister by four years, was a junior at Simmons College in Boston and was not overly alarmed about my health either. My siblings and I had never experienced any serious illness, and we naturally did not anticipate one now.

As for my parents, they had been through transitions and changes all of their lives, and outside of this growing concern that they felt for me, their lives were blossoming. My father was achieving financial security, very important to the son of struggling immigrant parents. Through skill and tenacity he had developed a thriving business with many employees. He was proud to provide for his family as his own parents had been unable to provide for him. We moved from impoverished Newark to patrician Short Hills. By the time I was ten years old, I was living in the lap of luxury. I had my own room, with my own private bathroom, equipped with both a bathtub and shower stall. My room was large, all decorated in my favorite color, pink, complete with a luscious pink canopy bed. We lived in a truly fantastic house with a basement large enough for many parties and an indoor swimming pool, which kept us busy after school and on weekends.

Our life in Short Hills sounds elegant, I know, but for me (and Sondra as well), it required difficult adjustments. We had lived our early life in predominantly Jewish neighborhoods. I took for granted the fact that I always fit in. In the Short Hills school system, however, I was the only Jewish girl in the two fourth-grade classes, and for the first time in my life I was exposed to anti-Semitism. A number of the children said that they could not play with me because I killed their God. It made no sense to me, but I was nonetheless hurt by it. The years in Short Hills were not easy, happy, or carefree ones for me or Sondra, who had similar experiences with her classmates.

But for my father, the house was wonderful, a symbol of the security and life-style he never had. Everything in his adult life was flowing just as he wanted it to, and he felt powerful and in control. I knew this, and that my mother shared his happiness. I wanted to do nothing to endanger it.

As winter turned to spring, however, I found it more difficult to cover up my illness. My symptoms became more frequent and severe. I began to double over from pain that deeply laced into me and did not pass so quickly. My parents were alarmed. My mother made an appointment with Dr. Marvin right away.

I remember the day prior to my appointment quite clearly. Toward the afternoon my mother nervously explained to me that I could not partake in the family barbecue as I was allowed only a liquid supper, with no food or water at all after twelve midnight. To make matters worse, before I went to bed I had to take two tablespoons of castor oil. I obeyed reluctantly, not anticipating that in two hours I would wake to spend the rest of the night running to the bathroom. In the morning I was tired and drained. I was shocked when my mother came into my room, this time carrying an enema, which she said I would have to use, doctor's orders. We argued back and forth as I sought desperately for a way out. "Your bowels have to be completely empty," she explained, "or the X rays cannot be done." "Completely empty? Completely empty!" I wailed. "What do you think they are now, full?" I eventually surrendered. Upset and exhausted, we both arrived at the doctor's office.

My father accompanied us. He knew how difficult I could be about doctors, and how painful it would be for my mother to handle me alone. She would need his support, and I his firm hand.

At the office the sight of a trayful of long silver tubes sent waves of panic throughout my system. When I asked the nurse what they were for, she replied that they were for the doctor to look into my rectum. I took one more look at those tubes, thought about the idea of the doctor putting them into me, and ran. "Over my dead body," I yelled as I dashed in a panic to find my parents. Of course I was soon back in the examination room.

Dr. Marvin requested that I try to be mature as he rotated the table I was leaning over so that my head was down and my bare bottom was up in the air. I screamed as I felt the cold metal tube pressing its way into my body, shocked at my pain and humiliation. When it was over, I again ran to my parents and begged them to take me home now! But there was still more testing to do.

This time I was positioned on one of the X-ray tables in the back of the office. I expected to be given a glass of chalky barium and was shocked when I saw the nurse attach an enema bag to a pole close to the table. The next thing I knew the nurse was trying put the tube into me. I practically flew off the table and ran into the waiting room. Again the same scene ensued and I ended up back on the X-ray table with the tube inside me. I felt small, embarrassed, humiliated. For my bowels, which had been ill for almost a year now, the barium enema was irritating and painful. What a relief it was when I could at last empty my bowels of all the barium that had been shot into them. It was an even greater relief when I was told that the tests were done and I could dress.

At this point my father left my mother and me to meet with the doctor and hear his report. My mother looked nervous and worn as we waited. We felt impatient and anxious to hear what he had to say.

"Mrs. Perl," he said, "your daughter has ileitis, a disease of the small intestine, also known as Crohn's disease or regional enteritis. It is a chronic disease and we have no cure for it."

No cure? My mother looked crestfallen. "Are you saying, doctor, that there is nothing that you can do?" asked my mother. Dr. Marvin said, "We have some drugs that have been helpful in controlling the growth of the disease, but at this point in time we cannot cure it, although researchers are working diligently to discover a cure."

Somehow the reality of what he was saying couldn't sink in. "I just don't understand," my mother said, "surely there's got to be some way for my daughter to recover."

"In some cases," Dr. Marvin continued, "the disease goes into remission, and the patient can feel wonderful." Remission. We liked the sound of that. It was the only positive word we had heard yet.

"What does that mean?" my mother probed further. "Does it mean that Sheri can be well again?" A thread of hope, a crust of bread, we'd take anything!

"Not exactly," said the doctor. "Remission is a period in which the patient feels well but, in actuality, the disease still exists as it is not curable." It all sounded like a bunch of mumbo-jumbo to us. How could it be possible for this illness to just go on and on indefinitely? The doctor went on to say that in extreme cases surgery was an option, but was certainly not something that we should consider at this time.

Dr. Marvin placed me on a bland diet, eliminating fresh fruit, fresh vegetables, roughage of any kind, milk and all milk products, spices or condiments, and all fried foods. I was a picky eater to begin with; now it would be even harder for my mother to put together meals that would appeal to me. He also started me on drug therapy, beginning first with sulfa drugs in an attempt to control the spread of the disease, and codeine pills to help with the pain. By the time I returned to school, in early spring, I had a number of different pill bottles with instructions for taking some before meals, others after meals, some in the A.M. and some in the P.M. I didn't take any of it too seriously, relying upon my mother to keep it all straight. Dr. Marvin also insisted that we make an appointment with an associate of his in Manhattan, a man well known for his work with this disease. He felt it was essential that we confirm his diagnosis and treatment with another opinion. And so an appointment was made.

I didn't like this doctor very much. He seemed cool,

abrupt, and unsympathetic. He checked out my X rays, insisted on doing his own rectal examination (which of course caused another mini-ordeal for me), and then announced that he concurred with the diagnosis of Crohn's disease, as well as the present course of treatment. All he had to add was his opinion that I rest more, probably even give up my position as cheerleader, and accept the fact that I was a very sick girl. Ugh!

I found myself drifting further and further away from my high-school friends and into myself. It seemed that they had no idea of what my life was like anymore and, by contrast, their interests seemed trivial and superficial to me. Instead I developed my relationship with Steve, my boyfriend. He was in his freshman year at Colgate University in Hamilton, New York, and most nights would find me buried in my father's den where I was able to make use of a long-distance watts line, whiling the hours away. Talking to Steve gave me something to look forward to. I could pour my heart out to him, sharing the most intimate details of my illness, and he never seemed to mind or grow impatient. He always had a humorous way of looking at the situation, as well as something warm and comforting to say. Our conversations became the highlight of my life.

It was around this time that my sister became involved with a handsome young surgical intern. Barry Mankowitz possessed many attractive qualities. He was a sweet man, handsome and intelligent. He was also responsible, and incredibly clean-cut, and in 1968 those qualities were becoming a rarity. Barry not only impressed my sister but my parents as well.

He proposed marriage to Sondra six short weeks after he met her. She accepted, although she was confused about her feelings toward him. I always wonder about the forces that brought them together because of the enormous role Barry would play in saving my life.

By the fall of my senior year I found it impossible to maintain my activities as a cheerleader. At the first few football games of the season, I tried to get by, mouthing the words to the cheers, feeling too tired to jump and shout at the same time. Soon it became apparent that the jumping alone was too much for me. It was a sad day for me when I handed over my uniform and megaphone to an excited classmate. As my mother pulled into the school driveway to take me home (I was too upset to remain in school that day), I began to ask if it mattered anyway. I wondered how something as trivial as cheerleading could matter if one could get so sick. "Who cared?" I rationalized. I did!

By this time I was thinner, weaker, and living with even greater pain. Dr. Marvin had tried a variety of sulfa drugs, but none helped. The only pills that seemed to work were the pain killers, which I soon came to see relieved anxiety as well as pain. Unfortunately, even they were being rendered impotent by this monster that was growing in strength and power with each passing day.

It was Sondra who had the courage to speak honestly with me then. She and I had always been close and now, with Barry her finacé, she knew more facts about my illness than I. I was surprised to learn from her that Barry thought my illness was very serious, more serious than I wanted to believe. I wanted to believe that things couldn't get any worse. But then it happened.

It was all planned and meant to be a beautiful fun-filled weekend. Steve and I, leaving from Colgate, where I was visiting him, were to drive all the way to Killington, Vermont, where we would ski with Sondra and Barry. I was staying with Steve in a hotel in town as we were just beginning to become intimate together. In the morning I had my usual difficult time in the bathroom but experienced nothing out of the ordinary. We had some breakfast, threw our bags in the back of his car, and set off. We hadn't driven far before I had to run into a gas-station bathroom. I was shocked at the sight of the bright red blood that filled the toilet bowl, shocked and horrified. I pulled on my jeans and ran into Steve's car dumbfounded. I must have been white as a sheet as I managed to get out the words that something awful had happened. To my absolute surprise, Steve asked me if I had started bleeding. He always had an uncanny way of sensing what was going on with me. We talked about what to do and decided to continue with our journey in the hope that the bleeding would stop. To our dismay the situation was very much the reverse and we were stopping at gas stations the entire way to Vermont.

By the time we arrived at the hotel I had lost a lot of blood. I felt weak, drained, and discouraged. Sondra and Barry had not yet arrived and so we sat patiently in our hotel room waiting. When they finally arrived I told Barry about what had happened. "You probably just popped a hemorrhoid," Barry said. "It happens all the time." "Can that produce a good deal of blood?" I asked. "Absolutely," Barry answered. "Are you experiencing much pain?" "Nothing out of the ordinary," I answered. "Then let's go skiing," said Barry.

Steve and I shared an anxious look. Maybe I should be more descriptive, I thought, but then I could be overreacting. I decided to refrain from further explanation and try to pull myself together. Once at the lodge and outfitted with skis, Sondra and Barry disappeared and Steve and I headed for a lift line. Extreme weakness overtook me, and I felt unable to control my legs. I started slipping backward and glided into a woman who supported me while Steve rushed over. He managed to maneuver my dead-weight body to a chair inside the lodge. We eventually found a ride back to our hotel room, where I slid between the sheets of the bed, warming my body with as many blankets as we could find. It was there I remained as we waited for Barry to return.

When Barry arrived and took my pulse, he looked as if he'd seen a ghost. Immediate plans were made for our return home. By the time we arrived home the bleeding had stopped, however, and I spent the next two weeks in the hospital. The same old tests were run, producing practically the same results. It seemed impossible to all of us that the X rays could be exactly the same when the symptoms were so much worse.

Upon my release, Dr. Marvin decided to start me on a new drug that he felt might have a dramatic effect upon my disease. He explained that he hadn't yet introduced cortisone because it is a very powerful drug, and is accompanied by some side effects. Although my X rays didn't indicate a worsening of my condition, a hemorrhage and my testimony did. He felt that the drug was warranted now. He didn't elaborate about the side effects and, at the time, I wasn't particularly interested in hearing about them. I figured that if the drug could handle the disease, I could handle the drug. When the doctor handed me the prescription, he said that he thought I might start feeling a good deal better in a few days. I was hopeful.

I never experienced one day of improvement from the cortisone. The disease seemed to have an uncontrollable hold on me. It wasn't until Steve remarked in early December that I looked like a chipmunk that I noticed how round and distorted my face had become. The first side effect of the drug (moonface) was surfacing. Beyond the side effects—which grew to include unwanted facial hair, insomnia, and severe depression—the drug had no effect.

I was so terribly ill the evening of my sister's wedding that it is a wonder I ever made it down the aisle as her maid of honor. So much time and money were spent to make this night perfect and I could hardly bear it. My mother wore that worried look under her smile every time she glanced in my direction.

I spent most of Sondra's wedding night in a hotel room. As I lay in bed thinking of the party going on downstairs, I realized that my illness was taking over my life. Even the splendor of my sister's wedding had been trampled on.

Sondra's wedding was a turning point in my illness. Before, I was sometimes able to poke my head out from inside the clouds and see the sky; now the disease seemed to pervade everything. I could no longer ignore it or sweep it under the rug. The symptoms were too constant, the pain too great.

Shortly after Sondra's wedding we were visited by a friend of my father's. Keith Gonsalves, a charming British gentleman who lived on Grand Bahama Island, was associated with my father through business. During his visit he made a point of telling me about two of his friends who had been cured of arthritis by a healer who resided in England. He said that the healer was referred to as "the man in the sanctuary," and that he had no physical contact with his friends. The healing took place transatlantically, so to speak. Now I had always liked Keith very much, and I didn't think he would lie to me. However, at eighteen I was certain that I knew just about everything there was to know about life, and there was no way I was going to believe such ridiculous tales. I held firmly to the belief that medical science was the only sound way to pursue health.

The beginning of 1969 found us very desperate. That is probably what prompted the extreme action we took next. On the advice of Steve's mother, we made contact with a doctor in Manhattan. We were told that Dr. Leon had a marvelous reputation for handling intestinal problems and was noted for curing cancer of the colon. We still couldn't accept the notion that medical science wouldn't cure my illness. After one entire year of treatment by Dr. Marvin, my condition was certainly deteriorating. Maybe it was time we explored new possibilities. Didn't we owe it to ourselves to make sure that we had covered all the bases?

A couple of weeks later my mother took me out of school and we drove together into Manhattan in search of new answers. Dr. Leon's office was filled with old, sick-looking people. For a moment I wondered what I was doing there, but the reason was all too clear. I was probably sicker than all of them. When I was finally taken in to see Dr. Leon, I was sweaty and shaky. I feared that he would put me through all the same miserable tests again. I was relieved to discover that he didn't feel the need to do his own rectal examination, and was content to read my X rays, press on my stomach, and ask me questions. He seemed quite cheerful as he went about examining me. When I asked if he had actually cured colon cancer, he replied that that had been his father. I envisioned his father with a small magic potion that he kept locked away in a closet. A simple little potion. You drink it and you're cured! Would he, I wondered, share it with me now?

When Dr. Leon told us his idea, I was intrigued. He prescribed a liquid medicine that he wanted me to take a half hour before meals. He claimed that it would coat my intestines, preventing food from further irritating them, thus allowing them to heal. He said that he wanted me to continue all the other medications I was taking, and simply add this one to the herd. It sounded easy enough. He then gave me a shot of vitamin B_{12}. As he withdrew the needle from my arm, he looked at my mother and said, "You'll need lead shoes to keep her down now!" It sounded good. It meant nothing. As my mother drove sadly and hopefully home through the Lincoln Tunnel, I slept, my head resting on her lap.

Naïve as we were, we were not prepared for Dr. Marvin's reaction. He had seemed annoyed when we asked him for my X rays, but he was outraged at the idea of this new medicine. As far as he was concerned, it was unorthodox, unheard of, and he didn't even know what it was made of. None of his colleagues (who were among the most respected doctors in the field) would use such a potion in their practice and neither would he. He said there was no way he could go along with this, and that if I insisted on taking the new medicine, he would be forced to resign from my case.

We were in a quandary. We had come to trust Dr. Marvin. He was kind and caring and we felt close to him. More important, he trusted me. He responded to my complaints sympathetically and without judgment. I did not fully realize what a nice doctor he was. But all of this paled beside the truth, that my condition had grown progressively worse over the year, and maybe it was time for another doctor.

To this day I have never tasted anything so vile as Dr. Leon's magic potion. As I washed the taste away with a gulp of water, I prayed that the magic would do its trick. Well, it sure did something, but the trick was on me. After three days, my pain became more and more severe. My mother and I spent our days trying to get through to Dr. Leon's office, but the phone lines were constantly busy. By the time six days had passed, my abdomen was so distended that I looked as though I was nine months pregnant, and we were still unable to reach our doctor.

We called Barry. Whenever we didn't know where to turn, we called Barry. He and Sondra were living in a two-bedroom apartment just outside of Millburn Center, a ten-minute drive from our house. He said that he would stop by and see me that evening before going home from work. My mother and I realized how absolutely necessary his presence was, for in truth, he was now the only doctor on the case.

By the time Barry arrived my father was home. "What do you think, Bar?" my father asked. With a doctor for a son-in-law, my father was beginning to think he was a doctor, too. "It must be a blockage, right?"

Barry wasn't sure, but didn't like what he saw. He said that he was afraid that I may have perforated, in which case surgery would be necessary. I didn't know what *perforate* meant, but I figured that it meant that something inside of me had popped or ripped open. He said that he would have to take some X rays to be absolutely sure, but that one thing was certain. I was going to the hospital. I was disheartened. The thought of returning to that environment for even one minute gnawed away at me. I had no choice, Barry explained. X rays had to be taken.

Barry phoned his uncle, Dr. David Baum, and asked him to please meet us at the hospital. David, a surgeon of extraordinary talent and dedication, was a small, quiet likable man. Since the time of Sondra and Barry's engagement, David had become an affectionate family member and seemed to have a special soft spot in his heart for me. Maybe because he knew I was sick, or maybe he just plain liked me, but he always had a warm word for me and an extra hug. I always had appreciated his presence whenever the family got together and was comforted by the fact that he was a doctor. I was glad to know that he would be meeting us at the hospital.

After reading the X rays, both David and Barry thought that surgery might be indicated but they weren't certain. They wanted the opinion of a gastroenterologist before they made any moves. "We're just surgeons," Barry said. "We're not as qualified to read these X rays as a gastroenterologist is. They've read so many more of these than we have. We have to be sure." Barry and my father headed to the telephones to track down a gastroenterologist.

Naturally, they first tried to locate Dr. Marvin, who was obviously the most familiar with the case and would probably take me back as a patient, considering my predicament. To our dismay, we discovered that he was out of town on vacation, and would not return for another week. Then, on the advice of Barry and David contact was made with Dr. Larry Timmons, the one doctor who should be glad that his name has been changed in the book. He showed up at the hospital about thirty minutes later. He was a tall slender man with pockmarked skin and dark brown piercing eyes. He looked at me accusingly, disappeared to read the X rays, and then arrogantly announced that surgery was not necessary. In a cold, hard, authoritative tone, he said that the new medication I was taking had obviously caused a blockage, which would disperse of its own, now that I was no longer taking the medicine.

About this he was correct. About everything else he was dead wrong. He immediately sized up my situation and decided that what he had here was the typical case of the spoiled, indulged child who was having a good time at everyone else's expense.

He checked me into the hospital, naturally against my wishes. He then proceeded to embarrass me by giving me a rectal examination in front of five young male interns. He then, with a cold and harsh expression on his face, told me that he knew what I was up to. He said that quite obviously I could fool my mother, my father, and my boyfriend, but that I'd better watch out, because I couldn't fool him. He dismissed all my complaints as exaggerations, treating me with less respect than I would give an animal. On top of all my physical pain, I now felt completely abused and humiliated.

This was the most uncomfortable hospital stay I'd had yet. Along with Dr. Timmons's cruelty, I was much sicker. Every test and examination irritated my sore insides even more than they had before. Dr. Timmons ordered an entire X-ray series, which included the night-before laxative and the morning enema. The enema was not only an embarrassment now but a painful experience as well. I remember the anger rising in my chest as the nurses on my floor made fun of me, referring to me as a mama's baby, as I called out for my mother in fear and pain. Later, lying on the cold, hard X-ray table, I felt unbelievably small and humiliated, unable to get used to the experience of a barium enema. I could not get through the sigmoidoscopy without a shot of Demerol. Now that I think of it, it was a rare occurrence when I survived the day without a shot of Demerol.

My mother seemed to go through every painful experience with me, from the changing of the IV needle, to the daily blood tests, to the painkilling injections. We were somehow locked in this thing together, the situation bringing us closer all the time. While my father, Steve, Sondra and Barry, as well as my grandparents frequently visited my hospital room, it was my mother who spent an eternity with me. After a Demerol injection, we would engage in long conversations. I would become extremely talkative. We were more like friends than mother and daughter. More than that, we were like two lost friends, trying to find a light at the end of a very dark and ominous tunnel. Led always by an eternal optimism, we kept searching for an answer, a reprieve . . . anything.

The new set of X rays showed very little change. How could the disease feel so much worse, and yet not appear worse when X-rayed? I was depressed, and what was worse, this news fit Dr. Timmons's warped opinion of me. He now knew, as he unkindly expressed, that I had a mild case of ileitis, because the X rays showed that a six-inch segment of small bowel was affected. He also knew that such a mild case could in no way produce the pain that I was complaining about. The time had come for me to shape up and stop driving everyone crazy. While we were all growing to hate Dr. Timmons, we had no guarantee that Dr. Marvin would take the case back and we couldn't imagine starting all over again with a new doctor.

Upon my release from the hospital I was sicker, weaker, and thinner than ever. Steve's visits became more important to me, while my sister and Barry were daily confidants.

Dr. Timmons decided to test me for ulcers and kidney problems. He found nothing wrong with my kidneys but decided to treat me for ulcers, just in case. For this, he prescribed an ounce of milk every hour. This was extremely shocking to my mother and me, as I had been denied milk and all milk products since the day ileitis had been diagnosed.

Twenty-four hours later I began to hemorrhage massively. There is no way of knowing whether the milk treatment was involved in bringing on the bleeding. My hunch is that I had it coming anyway, but the milk certainly couldn't have helped. Needless to say, the scene was terrifying. Again, the hemorrhage took the form of severe diarrhea, the only difference being that what poured out of me relentlessly was my own blood. At approximately two A.M. Dr. Baum arrived, took one look at the bright red blood in the toilet bowl, and explained that we had no choice but to check me into the hospital immediately.

The doctors began immediate blood transfusions in the hope of making me strong enough to withstand surgery. Doctors Baum and Mankowitz felt certain now that the only recourse was to go inside and remove the diseased portions of my bowel.

Up until now surgery had always seemed like an easy way out, if all else failed. I had grown used to hearing Barry say, "A chance to cut is a chance to cure," the surgeon's motto. But now, with the prospect of surgery so near, I began to wonder about the pain involved, realizing that I might get more than I had bargained for. Oddly enough, I had no concerns about dying. I assumed that I would live, but my concern was steadily growing about what I would feel like when I came out of surgery. Panic began to set in. I had a dread fear of pain. I began asking everyone around me if it was going to hurt, receiving my only answer from a friend of the family who was also a doctor. Stanley, who practiced gynecology, happened to be in the hospital and stopped in my room when he heard I had been admitted.

"Well, Sher," he said, "you know that when you cut your finger it hurts a little. You have to understand that this will be a somewhat deeper cut than a finger scratch. Naturally it will hurt some, but you'll be given something for the pain." At this point I knew that I was in for trouble.

The next few hours were spent getting me ready for surgery. I was in a state of complete terror, but was trying very hard to be strong. My parents and sister wiped my head and held my hands as the bag of blood, suspended above us on an IV pole, reminded us of the inevitable. Dr. Timmons arrived. A catheter was inserted into my bladder and my nightgown was cut away so as not to disturb my intravenous needles.

All that I could do was wonder about the pain. Could I bear it? I had had some pretty stiff pain, but I had the unerring sense that I hadn't seen nothin' yet. A few moments later I was rolled onto a stretcher, and before I knew what was happening, I was being swiftly wheeled down a corridor. My mother's hand was clasped tightly inside my own. She kept pace with the stretcher, her face glued to mine as she accompanied me as far as she was allowed. We parted ways at the big green doors marked "Operating Rooms—No Admittance." My mother bent over and kissed me. Then the ominous big green doors opened to admit me and I was wheeled away.

I lay on the stretcher for a while. I was a little groggy from sedation, but I knew what was going on. I saw other stretchers lining the hallways, also equipped with patients who were lying quietly. I was alone. Fear rose up inside of me, only partially subdued by the medication. "Why am I alone?" I thought. "Why can't my mother be here with me?"

A few minutes later I was wheeled into a room. A group of doctors and nurses helped me to maneuver my body off the stretcher and onto the table. "Where is David?" I thought. As I turned my head I saw him walking toward me. "David!" I said. "I'm scared, David." "I know you are," he answered. "Hold my hand, please, David," I said. As the anesthesiologist announced that he was inserting sodium pentathol into the IV in my arm, David told me that I was going to have a nice restful sleep soon. I quickly looked around the room and saw Barry's face. "Thank God," I thought. Another source of security and comfort. "Count backward from one hundred, Sheri," David said. I don't remember much past ninety seven.

Anesthesia is an odd thing. You can be under for hours, and yet at the first inkling of awareness, it feels as if no time has elapsed at all. I have this vague memory of feeling something inside my throat and a voice saying, "Well, she's coming to, better close her up." I don't know if I had become semiconscious during surgery, or if that was a dream. What I do know for certain is what I felt like as my senses began to come back to me in the recovery room. I felt as if the entire earth was sitting upon my abdomen. I never knew such pain could be possible, let alone endurable. "Oh my God," I thought, "I don't think I can deal with this." It hurt to move my toe. It hurt to move my pinkie. My mouth was incredibly dry and my throat hurt. My head throbbed, while my abdomenal pain was beyond imagination. I kept trying to go back to sleep, hoping to escape through dreams, but the pain kept jutting into my awareness.

Within a few minutes my mother was at my side. I could feel her pain almost as acutely as I could feel my own. I don't think I have ever loved her more than at that moment. The sight of her gave me courage. Her love convinced me, without words, that I would be able to stand all that I had to in order to get well. Her presence willed me to live. What a powerful and wonderful force love is!

My mother explained to me that Dr. Timmons had apologized. He had walked out of the OR in the middle of the surgery and announced to the members of my family that he had been wrong, that the surgery proved I had a far more extensive case of ileitis than the X rays ever revealed. I felt enormous satisfaction hearing this. "You see," my mother said, "your illness was extensive and there was real reason for your pain. Now that it has all finally been removed you are going to heal."

Although my mother did not mention this to me, Dr. Timmons also stated, rather abruptly, that Dr. Baum had to consider whether to perform an ileostomy. My family was shocked. Although they knew very little about ileostomies, they did know that it meant wearing an appliance on my body for the collection of waste materials. They couldn't imagine how I would ever adjust to such a situation and were greatly relieved to hear that Dr. Baum had decided to perform a resection instead. (In the case of the latter, the diseased portions of the bowel are removed, the healthy pieces are joined, and the bowel is reconnected normally.) Although in retrospect I realize that Dr. Timmons meant to inform my family of what was taking place in the OR, during what turned out to be a four-and-a-half-hour surgery, he only frightened my family further.

The next few days were a haze of pain and discomfort. I spent one night in intensive care in which I was aware of other beds around the room, some enclosed in oxygen tents. I heard people crying and begging for painkillers and I found myself trying to find the strength to do the same. It seemed as though the nurses' only reply was that I wasn't due for a shot for another two hours. I'd just have to wait. "Just wait?" I thought. "How could I wait?" Each minute of pain seemed like an eternity. I watched the clock on the wall endlessly, always amazed that more time hadn't elapsed. When the nurse finally came to my bedside with a needle, pulling myself over on my side to expose my backside was agony. Ah, but after those first few minutes, when the drug takes effect and the pain begins to dull, you know it has all been worth it, and you relish whatever relief you are given.

I remember that as soon as I was settled in a private room, my mother came and told me that Steve, who had been staying around the hospital waiting to see me, wanted to see me now. Sick as I was, the first thing that I thought of was the huge clump of knots that had formed in the back of my long brown hair during all the sweating, tossing, and turning of the last two days. We had tried to comb it out but it looked as though we would have to cut it. I decided that I looked terrible and that I didn't want to be seen in such a state. I needed to see Steve, but couldn't bear the thought of shocking him. "No," I told my mother, "tell him he can't come in. Tell him I don't want him to see me like this."

My mother left the room to give Steve my message, but returned immediately. Steve was not about to stand for any of this. "He wants to come in," she said. "He loves you, he wants to see you." A moment later Steve stood by my bed, gently stroking my hair, assuring me that I never looked more beautiful than at that moment. There was no question in my mind that I was loved.

I had severe discomfort in my throat and ear from a tube going into my right nostril and down my throat. My nurse explained that this Levine tube drained the bile and bodily fluids, which my intestines presently could not digest. It is, in actuality, a very helpful, and in many cases necessary tool in recovery from bowel surgery, but at this point my only interest in it was to get it out! My ear and throat throbbed continuously, and I was allowed only an occasional ice chip for the dryness. My doctors told me that the tube couldn't be removed, nor could I have anything to drink until I began to pass gas or have bowel movements, which could take a few days. I couldn't believe that we were all sitting around waiting for me to fart. Physiological functions had always been a private matter to me. Now mine were the business of the entire seventh-floor nurses' station!

My family practically lived in the hospital along with Steve, who faithfully came to see me every day. Flowers came by the cartful, with telegrams and gifts galore, but this was one time I couldn't muster a smile.

Each day I was experiencing increasingly worse gas pains. From what I was told, I understood that David had done a lot of cutting into my intestines in order to remove the disease. Because the disease was not isolated but was spread throughout my intestines in patches, David had to cut, remove, and sew back together all the healthy tissue that remained. Therefore many places in my intestines were swollen as a result of cutting and stitching. This made even the slightest act of functioning difficult. The pain was unnerving. David explained to me that painkillers, while valuable in one way, could also hurt my progress in another. They slowed down bowel function and could delay the time in which my bowels would work again. So, in essence, he was telling me to take as little pain medicine as possible and bear as much of the pain as I could.

Finally, on the seventh day I began to pass gas. We practically passed out flyers throughout the hall! I felt enormous relief, physically and mentally, as I now assumed that I was on my way to recovering, and putting all of this misery behind me.

Once the Levine tube was removed, I was going to walk down the hall with my nurse and actually take a bath! I would still be connected to an IV pole, but that didn't compare to the relief of being free of the catheter and Levine tube. The very thought of immersing my sore, sweaty body in warm caressing water sounded wonderful. The pleasure, however, was short-lived. When I returned to bed I began to experience bad cramps again. My intestines, for whatever reason, stopped functioning and I began to feel nauseated. Five minutes later, I was throwing up and running a fever. Barry and David were alarmed, and I was distraught. Down went the Levine tube—it's much less fun when you're awake—and immediate X rays were ordered.

Fortunately, the X rays showed that nothing had gone wrong with the surgery. My present difficulties were the result of an infection and I was spared the agony of another operation. Yet I can't really say that things were looking up.

I had severe abdominal cramps. The Levine tube felt as if it were burning a hole in my neck and ear. I was weak beyond belief, and I was sore and aching from head to toe. But "Thank God," I thought, "at least I don't have to go into surgery again."

The next few days were a long and tiresome waiting game. We had to wait until the antibiotics killed the infection enough for my bowels to begin to work again. Then and then alone could the Levine tube be removed, and I be allowed a little bit of water. How I wanted water.

As the days passed I watched a lot of television. The image that remains clearest in my mind from all the hours of TV is from a soft-drink ad—A bottle of soda sitting in the center of a cool stream of rushing water. I couldn't tell which looked more refreshing, the stream or the bottle. I longed to devour them both. I'll never forget what it feels like to be so thirsty and not have the freedom to take a drink. To this day it is a great pleasure for me to take a glass, fill it to the brim with ice, pour cool refreshing liquid over the ice, and drink it to my heart's content. It was then that I learned that the simple pleasures of life, which are usually taken for granted, come into sharp focus when they are taken away.

Once my bowels began to work I was in for another kind of trouble. I had intense diarrhea and could barely get off the bed to use the portable commode by the bedside. Moving my body still caused great pain. I had a bad case of hemorrhoids, and I could barely use my own hands to clean myself because they were all rigged up to IV needles. With one nurse to hold me and another to clean me, I felt completely humiliated and small. But basically, things had taken a step in the right direction. With great relief I gave up the Levine tube and was allowed small amounts of liquids. With great effort I went for small walks down the hall and sat up in a chair. Steve and I engaged in Dr. Timmons jokes, the resulting laughter creating as much pain as pleasure. The general tone in my flower-cluttered room was improving as my situation seemed to move out of the critical stages.

The two months discussed in this chapter seemed to me like two years. Therefore it was only natural that when I was drinking, eating, and using the bathroom frequently, but without pain, I started to grow anxious to go home. Doctors Baum and Mankowitz both agreed, and signed the release form. Dr. Timmons took a little more persuading, but eventually he gave in.

I felt as if I'd been let out of prison on the warm sunny morning that I left the hospital in Newark. I had been admitted on a cool winter's night, and during my stay, without my awareness of it, winter had mysteriously turned into spring. And what a glorious spring day it was. Everywhere was green, everything smelled sweet, freedom never felt so good!

My dog Mitzy, who my mother said faithfully checked the house throughout the day for my presence, returning always to my bedroom, was delighted to see me as we both climbed into my soft luscious pink canopy bed. It was good to be home. Although I was still quite weak, it seemed as though the ileitis disease had actually been removed. The daily pain was gone, and although I still had to make frequent bathroom visits, I was no longer suffering. I weighed a mere sixty pounds and was covered with black and blue bruises from the enormous number of shots and intravenous needles. But that would all change. The illness was gone and the hellish ordeal was behind me.

- 3 -

The Trauma Continues

It wasn't until I was home and life was getting back to normal, that I learned of the severity of my operation and of the type of surgery that had been considered for me and decided against by Dr. Baum. Sondra explained that David, who is known for his calm and quiet manner, found himself in an emotional state that was almost overwhelming. Shocked to discover such extensive bowel disease inside me, he was faced with the serious decision to perform either an ileostomy or a resection. Sondra explained that in the case of an ileostomy, a piece of my intestine would be brought through my abdominal wall and I would eliminate waste through it. Unable to make the decision, Dr. Baum made a phone call in the middle of surgery to an associate of his in Manhattan. Dr. Arnold told David that he was thinking with his heart and not with his mind, and that in his opinion a temporary ileostomy should be performed. (With a temporary ileostomy the rectum remains intact, thus allowing for the reconnection of the bowel at some later date.) I guess because David and I were so close, he could not help but think with his heart, and therefore could not bring himself to perform an ileostomy on me. Thus the resulting surgery was a resection.

How shocking this story sounded to me at the time, and how awful! "I would rather be dead," I told my sister, and I believed it to be true. Imagine me walking around with a bag under my clothes collecting waste! I shuddered at the thought.

About two weeks later I started to hemorrhage again. The same old routine, the bloody runs. I was rushed to the hospital, transfusions were begun, and the waiting game was on to see if the bleeding would stop. This time it did, and after a few days I was sent home. We were all very shook up about this, however, as we had thought that my problems were over.

On a trip to the Bahamas with my parents, a vacation David had approved of, I was waiting in the beauty parlor for my mother when a trip to the bathroom confirmed the start of bleeding again. We panicked. To our relief the bleeding stopped within a few hours, but the anxiety remained. The bleeding was alarming and disconcerting, like a time bomb always ticking away. We never could be sure whether it was going to go off again or of the severity of it, if it did. I was supposed to be well—but was I really?

That June I was determined to attend my senior prom with Steve. I felt as if I had been forgotten by all of my classmates and I wanted to make my presence known, to let people know that I still existed. They couldn't understand what I had been going through, I reasoned, but at least they could see that I had survived!

My mother, in whose eyes I now was a china doll, was uneasy. She would have preferred it if I didn't move a muscle. She pleaded with me to stay at home and rest and not push myself. "Honey," she said, "let yourself have a chance to heal." She was so upset that I could not have gone with a free heart. I granted her wish and decided to pass on the prom. Unfortunately, my mother's fears were not groundless. She was trying to prevent the inevitable, but then is the inevitable ever preventable?

The very next day, while shopping with my mother and sister in Bloomingdale's, I began to hemorrhage again. After a few trips to the Bloomingdale's bathroom, we nervously made our way to my mother's car, eventually ending up in Dr. Timmons's office. I knew that I was in trouble because I just couldn't stop running to the bathroom. "God," I thought, "just stop this, now! Please!" But my blood rushed through me like a river. And oh God, I knew what was next. Dr. Timmons said that we had no other choice but to return to the hospital, and this time I didn't even bother to try to convince anyone otherwise.

I knew that more surgery was a strong possibility, given

the severity of this hemorrhage. I was doubly concerned now, for I remembered what my sister had told me about ileostomies. It didn't take a hell of a lot of brains to deduce that if I had to go into surgery again, I might very well end up with one. I just didn't know if I could make the adjustment.

At the hospital Dr. Timmons ordered a coagulant, in enema form, in an attempt to try to stop the bleeding, hoping to avoid another surgery. Unfortunately the treatment had no effect and the bleeding continued full force.

I now realized that, again, I was dealing with a fight for survival. It also became clear to me, under those circumstances, that I would accept whatever situation was thrust upon me in order to survive.

Nothing was more obvious to me then than the fact that I wanted to live even if that meant adjusting to an ileostomy—the thought of which still made me shudder. I also realized, at the same time, that I could not allow myself to indulge in too much thought about the ileostomy, for I sensed that I needed all my energy to survive the surgery. It's not as if I consciously realized this, but I somehow knew not to dwell upon it. I tried to summon up all my courage as the emergency preparations were begun to make me ready for my second surgery.

An immediate blood transfusion was started, but this time with greater difficulty. Because my veins were so worn from overuse during my last surgery, Barry could not find a suitable vein to administer the blood through. Therefore he was forced to perform a minor surgical procedure in the crook of my arm, in order to place a needle in a vein deeper than surface level. Everybody around me looked panicky. David stopped in briefly, said he'd see me in the OR, and disappeared into the hall. Everything seemed to be moving too fast. As I was whisked down the corridor to the operating room, my mother running alongside the stretcher, I knew what I was up against. I looked up into my mother's face, my mind teeming with questions. "Mommy, will I be a whole girl when I come out?" I asked. I must have torn a hole in her heart by asking. "Whatever you will be, you will be alive, and you will be beautiful, and you will get well!" she answered.

When I awoke in the recovery room I saw Barry, who was standing just behind the head of my bed. I somehow knew the answer before I asked him if the ileostomy had been done, to which he replied, "Just for a little while, Sher." The pain was as bad as I had remembered it. The dryness in my mouth and irritating Levine tube were present again also. I knew that I was in no way ready to look at my body in its present state; nevertheless I kept picturing it. I couldn't imagine how I would ever adjust. To my mind, the idea of moving one's bowels through one's abdomen was disgusting. I became obsessed with ways to disguise the bag, which I hadn't even looked at yet.

Steve was helpful beyond measure. He came to my bedside, placed his hands on my belly, and said that he could not hate anything that gave me back to him. When many young men would have walked away, he walked in. His parents also lent support, holding to the belief that now my bowel could have the rest that it required. We all maintained that, as soon as it was possible, the ileostomy would be reversed.

My own parents were heartbroken, although they tried not to show it. How this could have happened to their daughter was beyond them. I couldn't imagine how I would ever make the adjustment. My once perfect body, which I had been too young and foolish to appreciate, seemed mutilated. I felt as if I was now marred, in an unforgivable way. Again I sensed the need to ignore this wave of negative thought and reasoning. It was as if a portion of myself, which knew better, fought to pool all my resources for immediate use. Again this proved very necessary, as the recovery from the second surgery was every bit as eventful as the recovery from the first.

To begin with, as before, there was a problem with the functioning of my bowel. We were anxious for my bowel to begin working, indicating that the surgery had been successful, and that the hated Levine tube could be removed. Unfortunately, this was not the case and the little plastic bag my nurse had tied around my belly remained empty. There was no sign of the passing of fluids through my body into the bag. Soon I became nauseated.

I remember that my mother and I were in the hospital

room with one of my nurses. Periodically throughout the day it would be her job to drain the Levine tube. This entailed using a suction device to draw out any excess fluid, thus assisting the tube in its function. As I became overwhelmed with waves of nausea I told my mother, who in turn told the nurse, who in turn looked at the machine connected to the other end of the Levine tube and answered, "The machine is working."

"Well, it may be working," my mother said, "but my daughter is very nauseous. I think it would be best if you would please drain the tube!"

"No," she answered, "the machine is working!"

"Ma!" I said, "do something."

My mother grabbed the suction device and a bowl and began to drain the tube herself. She must have filled the bowl up four times with my bodily fluids, affording me enormous relief and warning us that something was not right.

The nurse called for an intern, who, after putting his ear to my stomach, contacted my regular doctors. X rays were then done in my room by a portable machine, because I was considered too weak to be moved. The X rays showed that my intestines had coiled themselves up into some kind of knot and that was why they were not yet able to function.

The next thing I knew, Barry walked into the room briskly with some kind of ball in his hand. I could see that he was trying to press it into as small a shape as possible and then, before I knew what was happening, he pushed it into my one free nostril back as far as he could, saying, "Swallow, swallow, swallow." I felt shocked for an instant and then saw that Barry was feeding a tube, appearing at this point just like a Levine tube, slowly into me. He explained that the ball that was on the end of the tube was a ball of mercury, the weight of which was going to go through my intestines and break up the coil. I was to alternate every half hour from lying on one side to the other, assisting the tube in going through my intestines.

After two hours of turning from side to side, an X ray revealed that the tube had merely coiled into a knot itself, and so the entire process had to be started again. Fortunately, this time it was successful. By the end of the day we began to see fluid passing into the clear plastic bag on my abdomen, which upset me as much as it pleased me. Now, for the first time, I dared to look at this contraption that was my body, and I cringed with shock and dismay. It looked as though I had a red cherry growing out of where my belly button should be, with a clear plastic bag placed over it and tied around my body with a string. I also discovered another red, cherrylike opening lower down on my left side, near my groin, which Barry said was the temporary. I really had no idea what he meant except that, because of it, I could be rehooked again at some later date.

My mother and I both recall that, at this point, Barry had said something to the effect that there had not been enough large bowel left to make a proper temporary hook-up, and that David had invented an unusual solution in order to make my situation reversible. I didn't understand what he was talking about. The ileostomy was *temporary*, which meant to me that I would endeavor to get rid of it as soon as possible. Until it was gone, I didn't care to know anything about the details beyond how to live with the situation now.

By this point my bowels were working and the little bag was filling up constantly with my bodily fluids. The nurses took one bag off me, replacing it with another, while I watched, detached from my own body.

My next complication was a high fever. Since my bowels were working, indicating that the surgery had been successful, it was assumed that I had another infection. This time the antibiotic had to be administered by injection, which was what I feared, because of the pain involved. To make matters worse, I would have to have the shot twice a day, and what a shot it was! Barry said it might sting a little as he proceeded to inject me with a serum so painful that I cried for ten minutes. All in all, life just seemed to be one miserable, painful event after another.

It was at this time that a woman came onto my case whose presence was more than helpful. Ruth Kale, a fine postsurgical (as well as general) nurse, was approached by David and asked to take the case, since my current nurse felt that she could no longer stand the pressure. Ruth, who told me herself during an interview I held with her in 1987 (the first time we had seen each other in seventeen years) that she always liked a challenge, came on to the case with zest and determination. She also had a good deal of practical knowledge about ileostomies and was not afraid of getting her hands wet. She informed me, as she entered my room, that she was referred to around the hospital as the shit nurse, because she handled so many of these problems. I felt immediate embarrassment when she said that, but it was obvious that she did not look at my situation as unusual or terrible. Waste to her was a natural part of life, and just something else to be dealt with, where to me it represented something to be ashamed of.

Ruth's attitude, so healthy and accepting, began to set the groundwork for my being able to cope. I knew that soon I was going to have to learn how to take care of this thing myself, and that meant approaching my fear of looking at and touching my body. I had an enormous aversion to it but Ruth didn't. She explained to me that once I had healed from the surgery I would be able to use much nicer appliances that fit better and looked far nicer than the temporary ones I was using now. I couldn't imagine any kind of appliance that wouldn't be horrendous.

In part I realized that this was me now, that I had to find a way to accept it, and that I could, and that I would. Yet, in another part, I couldn't accept it at all, and I didn't even want to try. I could feel my moods swing back and forth, from one extreme to the other. From feeling sorry for myself, to feeling glad to be alive, I somehow began to set myself off in the direction of accepting my present reality.

I was also greatly relieved to discover that Ruth, who had a special skill for giving injections, could administer my antibiotic painlessly. It was really just a matter of taking a little more time, which I realize most doctors and nurses don't have. A terrible ordeal became an ordinary event. Believe it or not, my uncle Bernie drove Ruth back to the hospital every evening to administer the medication during another nurse's shift, because nobody could do it like Ruth. At this point, it seemed as though every member of my family would have done anything to save me from pain.

I was surprised to learn from Ruth that, on the day she walked on to my case neither she nor the doctors felt that I would pull through, and that Dr. Baum expressed his concern to her often. "It's a good thing," my mother said (also present at the interview), "that he didn't tell me what he was thinking."

For my next act, I developed a frightening complication. It was frightening because my doctors were not certain as to the cause of my alarming symptoms. According to Ruth my blood pressure was dropping, my hemoglobin was down, my fever had shot up, and the doctors were afraid for my survival. My mother said that this remains in her mind as the most terrifying of all the times of my illness because she was beginning to feel that we just might lose the fight. She saw real fear in the doctors' faces, and she felt that I was losing my sense of reality.

Once blood tests were run and analyzed the mystery was solved. I had developed an electrolite imbalance due to excessive fluid loss through the ileostomy. Apparently when my bowels began to work, they worked overtime. We, however, did not know what to expect from my bowels and, therefore, no one was aware that I was losing too much fluid. Now that we realized the cause of my problem, another IV was inserted into a vein in my shoulder and the necessary electrolytes were administered.

That night, at my request, I was given some strong medication and I finally slept through the night. When I awoke in the morning I felt a good deal better. My mother seemed genuinely shocked when I told her how much better I felt. I could not understand why she seemed so surprised. At the time I had no notion of what my family was going through. As difficult as reality was, to my mind death was not a possibility. The main issue to me was when the suffering would stop.

I came through this last complication and began to heal. I was now faced with the difficult task of adjusting to the ileostomy and yet, at this point, the actual fight for survival came to an end.

Learning to accept and adjust to the ileostomy was no easy task. Ruth Kale was vitally helpful. She touched my body and the fluids came out of it without any hesitation or sense of disgust. She was as natural and comfortable with it as I would have been petting a puppy. Her attitude demonstrated to me that I didn't have to be afraid of what I was, and that my squeamishness could be overcome, but I knew it wasn't going to be easy.

Finally, I was released from the hospital. Although incredibly thin and worn, I was alive, and relieved to be out of pain. I began to recover my strength quickly in my home environment. Steve was unbelievably wonderful as he showered me with gifts and affection. Truly he helped, almost more than anyone, to make my adjustment bearable. The fact that he remained my boyfriend, refusing to run away from the situation, was positive proof that I was still desirable. He was much less squeamish about the ileostomy than I was. He clearly didn't seem offended. To me his attitude seemed nearly unbelievable. I was so narrow-minded at eighteen, so prissy and set in my ways, that I couldn't imagine physically loving someone who was in my situation. How he could continue to love me was a mystery to me. My attitude toward myself had changed radically. I now looked down on myself as someone unworthy.

I was in enormous emotional pain, which I tried to conceal. On the surface it looked as if I was doing okay, making the necessary adjustments and continuing with my life. Underneath, however, there was a profound sadness. I was determined not to let it show. I acted as if I were much less upset than I was. I even advised other ostomates on how to get back on their feet, physically and emotionally, and yet I had not done so myself. As I look back on it now, helping others and pretending that I wasn't so miserable made my adjustment easier. Clearly, I wasn't yet ready to face the enormous shock and hurt feelings that resided just below surface level. Although I was aware that I was sad and disappointed, it was not until years later that the deep wounds inflicted by my illness were acknowledged and allowed to heal.

I was very fortunate that my schoolteachers and principal decided to graduate me and, with a little help from my guidance counselor, I was accepted by a local university. This way I could attend college in the fall and still live at home. The idea of living at home didn't thrill me, but I didn't know how I could share a bathroom with other girls. I couldn't imagine telling other people that I had an ileostomy, or worse, having them see it.

At this point my mother, sister, and I spent what seemed to be an eternity in the bathroom trying to get an appliance on me that felt comfortable. We were unaware that I had a constriction problem (my abdominal wall grew tighter and tighter around the exposed piece of intestine, called the stoma), and therefore interpreted the constant itching I experienced as the result of an ill-fitting appliance. We tried everything we could think of to make me more comfortable. We were constantly taking the appliance on and off, adjusting the fit, and applying different creams and ointments. However, within a short time after leaving the bathroom, I became uncomfortable.

At this point my operation was a deep, dark secret that I confided only to one friend besides Steve. Even my younger brothers were kept in the dark, as my parents shared my belief that my operation was not something to be talked about. After a while my brothers began to wonder what my mother and I were doing in the bathroom all of the time. Eventually I sat down and explained the situation to Richard, who, like everyone else, accepted it better than I did.

As soon as possible, I made trips with my mother to Philadelphia to see a gastroenterologist chosen by Dr. Baum, to consult on when to go back into surgery to close the bowel. We made three visits, and I was subjected to some of my very favorite tests.

I clearly remember the jealousy I felt as my mother and I traveled home from Philly in early June, stuck in bumper-to-bumper traffic while carfuls of young people drove to the Woodstock festival. How I envied them and their freedom to be on their own without parents and doctors. Although my illness insulated me from the minds of other young people throughout the country, I nevertheless sensed something in the air. It was clear in the music I listened to, and I wanted a taste of it. In my own quiet way, I felt a part of the movement.

I spent the summer regaining my strength and weight, lounging around the pool in my parents' home, and going out with Steve.

I was pleased when he decided to spend his junior year in Manhattan, at NYU, as part of an exchange program. I felt safe knowing he would be around. He rented a small apartment in Greenwich Village, which has always been my favorite part of Manhattan, and with the prospect of reconnective surgery in the future, life seemed better.

Although I was very uncomfortable about having sex, and extremely ill at ease about taking my clothes off, Steve and I did have an intimate relationship. He was patient and understanding with me, loving and supportive. He was just what I needed, which made it all the more difficult for me to accept what happened next.

In the early fall Steve informed me that he needed to date other women. Fear rocked my body as I listened to his justifications. My emotions raced from rage to sadness, to disbelief, to fear, and I begged Steve to reconsider. I knew that he loved me and I hoped to play on his sympathies, but Steve was unshakable. Naturally, I was certain that his new attitude had to do with the ileostomy. Although he tried to convince me otherwise, I couldn't believe him.

I was scared, annoyed, bored, disinterested, and upset when I drove into the parking lot of Drew University for freshman orientation. I had no idea what I was doing there. I missed Steve terribly. I was afraid to date other men, knowing that they would eventually want to get sexual and I would have to tell them about my body. I couldn't bear another rejection, and I couldn't imagine that it wouldn't come about. I just wanted to go to sleep and wake up in the morning to find that it had been a dream.

Fortunately I began to develop friendships with some of the local kids who, like myself, had not gone away to school. That created a social outlet for me and saved me from dealing with the pressure of dating. It helped my self-confidence to be socializing with people my own age.

Sometime during this fall my gastroenterologist announced that my bowel appeared to be healed and that now seemed as good a time as any to reconnect it. He explained that if the surgery was not successful, I would have to accept a permanent ileostomy, but that at this point in time we should hope for the best.

I was very excited as my mother and I stopped off at my father's office on the way home from Philadelphia to give him the news. To my surprise, my father was not very pleased at the prospect of my facing another surgery and said so. I was shocked and disappointed that he didn't share my enthusiasm. Nevertheless, I was headstrong and headed over to David's home that evening to tell him the good news. My heart sank when David said that he refused to do the surgery at this time. "You just aren't well enough," he said, "and I don't believe that your body can withstand another surgery right now."

I couldn't believe my ears. Furthermore, I was outraged that he had sent me to a specialist, had allowed me to go through so many dreaded examinations, if he didn't intend to operate anyway. As I drove home I was sad and disillusioned, but I also felt a surge of relief. Could it be that I wasn't really ready to face another surgery yet?

Things did continue to improve in some ways. Steve was having a hard time with our separation. He began to pursue me actively again. This time, though, I wanted some assurances. I felt that I needed some kind of formal commitment and pressured Steve for one.

We became engaged and planned to be married in early August. Both our families were very excited. Steve and I became so caught up that I don't really think we knew exactly what was happening. It seemed like the right thing to do. He didn't want to lose me, and I didn't want to face life alone, without him. We were both so young and had been through so much together that no other course of action seemed possible.

I felt free now to drop out of college, which was something I had wanted to do desperately. I found school tedious, and my courses difficult to concentrate upon. The only thing that seemed truly interesting to me was what I referred to as my new pot-smoking awareness. In keeping with my generation, I became very introspective and involved in discovering more about myself, my thoughts and my motives. I began to feel that I had to understand myself in order to understand what was happening around me. I started reading books about psychology, trying different theories on for size, to see which ones seemed valid.

Such pondering kept my mind active, while on a physical level I had plenty to do planning my wedding and engagement party. I no longer suffered pain, had fairly abundant energy, and outside of my annoying constriction problems, I seemed to be well. I smoked pot frequently and the marijuana slowed down my digestive process, which decreased the amount of trips I had to make to the bathroom, and increased my weight. I also discovered that pot distracted me from the constant itching that resulted from the constriction problem. Distraction, however, didn't solve the problem.

Two days before my engagement party my constriction problem made itself truly felt. We were expecting nearly two hundred people for a party at my parents' home when I suddenly got a case of the runs so severe that by that evening I was flat on my back. Dr. Baum came by and, to my dismay, tried to put his pinkie into the opening of the stoma and found that it was practically closed shut. My abdominal wall was growing together around the stoma, and thus I was experiencing severe fluid loss. The doctor explained that the diarrhea was a direct result of this partial blockage. The only way to stop the problem was to go into surgery and cut the overgrown skin away. He said that it would most likely be a minor surgical procedure. However, if for some reason he was not able to solve the problem from the outside, he would be forced to completely open me up again, which would qualify as major surgery. "Major surgery again?" I thought. "Please God not that!" And what, I wondered, were we going to do about the party?

We came up with an outrageous solution. That night Barry arrived at our home with an IV pole and all the equipment necessary to set up intravenous therapy for me in my bedroom. The plan was to replace all of the fluids I had lost while a strong constipating drug called parapectolin would be used to block the diarrhea condition until after the party. Then I would have the surgery. We had two days to get me into shape for the party, and we succeeded triumphantly. I looked healthy and fresh as a daisy, and when the guests arrived, no one would have thought that I had spent the last two days in bed.

The party went nicely from what I could tell, but as the day wore on I became more and more apprehensive about the impending surgery. I elected to discontinue the parapectolin because it made me drowsy, and within no time the diarrhea returned. By the time the last guest had left, I looked quite different from the way I had looked when the party began. Huge hollows appeared in my cheeks as my strength began to wane. I climbed into my bed and thought about the next day. I was looking at another surgery, the extent of which would remain a mystery until the actual event.

The moment that I opened my eyes in the recovery room, I knew that the surgery had been a minor one because I had minimal pain and I had no Levine tube in my nose. I breathed more than a sigh of relief!

In order to prevent future surgeries of this nature, Barry told me to dilate the stoma every day when changing the appliance. This meant putting my pinkie into the opening of the stoma and keeping it there for a few minutes. In this way I would be pushing the skin outward and working against the constriction process. The doctors said that they hoped this would work, and that if it didn't, we would just have to operate again. Sounded great to me!

Steve and I were excited about our upcoming wedding. My parents were planning a huge affair with six hundred people. We chose the Pierre Hotel in Manhattan and selected an elaborate meal. We were starting fittings for our gowns and the invitations were just about to be mailed when I surprised myself and my parents by announcing that I wanted something smaller and simpler. I said that I felt that such an enormous wedding was a waste of money. I was very outspoken and didn't realize at the time that I disappointed and hurt my parents. I was putting down their style and way of doing things. During the next few years, I became more and more critical of their values. I blamed them for my own confusion. I was quick to criticize what I saw as their materialistic values, but I had no problem about taking their money.

This was a difficult time for me. As I delved more deeply into psychology, I began to blame my past for my present difficulties. It was easy then to transfer the blame to my parents. It was only natural then for me to desire change, but I was unduly critical of them. You could say that I fit into my generation well, as all around me, young people bitched and complained about the world their parents had created.

Both sets of parents were disturbed by Steve's and my

behavior, but they agreed to go along with our plans. Looking back, I'm not sure that it mattered to Steve which wedding plan we followed, but I clearly wanted an event that reflected my changing values. As a result, the guest list was limited to a hundred people. Half of these were kids, which really limited our parents in the amount of people they could invite. Steve and I made our own invitations sporting a photograph of the two of us on the front. Inside we quoted Crosby, Stills, and Nash—"One person two alone three together for each other"—and one of my grandmothers wanted to know if it meant that I was pregnant. We wrote our own vows, and I bought myself an old-fashioned lacy dress in Greenwich Village. I was undoubtedly rude and arrogant, but I rejoiced in the feeling of running my own life.

We went apartment hunting and found a terrific apartment in a new housing development near Colgate University, where Steve would be starting his senior year in the fall. I stirred with excitement at the thought of living on my own for the first time in my life. I was actually more excited about that than about being married.

As I walked down the aisle on my father's arm I sensed that something in my relationship was missing. I didn't know what it was, and yet I longed for it. Still, Steve was the best thing in my life and I could not bear to be without him. This did seem to be the right move.

Whether my sister's marriage had been the best move for her was becoming questionable. It was all too apparent with me on my feet, that Barry and Sondra had little in common. As if they had been woven together for the sole purpose of seeing me well, they began to drift apart. Sondra grew more dissatisfied as time passed and she sensed the huge gulf between them. They were eventually divorced, and as I look back I can only feel tremendous gratitude toward both of them, for it was I who benefited most from their union.

My fall at Colgate University was deliriously happy. I was surrounded by people my own age, as our building housed mostly Colgate students. We became very friendly with three fellows who lived diagonally across the hall, and there were always parties or small get-togethers taking place. While some of us played guitars and sang, others watched ball games and played chess. Most everyone smoked pot. I found myself being drawn into spiritual discussions with my friends.

People were getting interested in Baba Ram Dass and tapes of him speaking were circulating around campus. He spoke of meditation and of the peace of mind that could be achieved through giving up the ego. This idea appealed to me because my ego was so inflated as a result of my ileostomy. I found it comforting to explore the spiritual rather than the physical plane, where, in my mind, I no longer made the grade.

I figured that in the spring or summer I would probably have surgery to reconnect by bowel, but I kept pushing the event into the future now, afraid to rock the boat. Little did I know that the boat was about to start rocking anyway.

- 4 -

My Second Illness

By the end of November the party came to an end. Toward the middle of the month I began to feel extremely weak, so much so that I couldn't ignore it. I soon felt mildly ill and experienced headaches. Before long it was overwhelming.

Steve and I were planning to come home for Thanksgiving break and so my mother made an appointment with—guess who—good old Dr. Marvin. After all this time, he had taken over my case again. Unfortunately, it seemed as though we would be needing his services again.

I couldn't believe how disillusioning it felt to be back in the doctor's office. It didn't seem possible that I could actually be ill again. Dr. Marvin was very sympathetic as he drew blood from my arm. He assured us that he would call as soon as he had some results.

When the doctor did call, he spoke to my mother. It appeared that I had hepatitis, but the doctor said that he did not see this as something to be overly concerned about. He explained that with proper bed rest and care the liver usually repairs itself. I was instructed to have monthly blood tests. The doctor felt that within six months' time I would probably be well.

There was no prescribed treatment beyond bed rest, but then nothing seemed more disturbing to me than the idea of being back in bed again. To make matters even worse, Steve made me promise to give up marijuana. We both felt guilty about it possibly playing a role in making me ill, and so I reluctantly agreed.

Of course my parents wanted me to convalesce at home, but I insisted upon returning with Steve to Colgate. I wasn't ready to surrender my newfound freedom. As the dishes and garbage piled up, however, I grew sadder and lonelier. All of my friends, busy and actively involved in their lives, only served to remind me of how pathetic my situation was. As I saw it, I was already badly disfigured by my ileostomy. It was unbelievable to me that I could actually be incapacitated again, this time by a sick liver. The cloud of illness that engulfed me never seemed to end. I began to agree with my parents that I might be better off at home.

I went back and forth between Colgate and home throughout the rest of the school year. I was frustrated, stopped in my tracks. I had just begun to spread my wings when I was forced to return to the nest again.

I had regular blood tests, always expecting to see change for the better, but as winter turned to spring we saw no improvement at all. Dr. Marvin grew concerned as the disease was not behaving as he had expected it to. He informed my parents that he was afraid that I might have the chronic form of hepatitis, which grows progressively worse. He insisted that I see a doctor, an associate of his in Manhattan, who specialized in liver illness.

A liver biopsy was done sometime in May. I was very frightened, as always, by the medical procedure. I found myself shaking as the specialist, after anesthetizing my right side with novocaine, somehow managed to extract a piece of liver through my skin. Like a scene from an old movie played over and over, my sister and mother rushed to my bedside to comfort me. None of us could believe the endlessness of this tunnel. The doctor said we would have the results in about a week, and that until then he could tell us nothing.

During this time my mother gave me a copy of *The Search for Bridey Murphy* in the hope of taking my mind off things. It was about a woman who under hypnosis remembered an existence in another lifetime. I was completely fascinated by the concept and through the book was introduced to the gifted psychic, Edgar Cayce. I quickly purchased a few of his books and found myself enthralled and excited by what I read.

Cayce, who had never read any book in his life except the Bible, could go into a trance state in which he would speak fluently in medical terms. He would make diagnoses and prescribe cures. Known as the Sleeping Prophet, he was sometimes called in on medical cases when doctors were unable to determine the cause of a given problem. He even delved into the past lives of his patients, clarifying their present situations through his perceptions of their past.

I was deep into Cayce when the biopsy results came back. They showed conclusively that I had the chronic form of hepatitis, which was all the more dangerous, my doctors explained, because they couldn't operate on the liver. Unlike my last disease when we had been able to cut away diseased portions of my intestines, we were now powerless. The doctors saw no way to stop this disease from consuming my liver. They did not tell me, but my parents understood, that this could be fatal.

I didn't fully comprehend the seriousness of what was happening. Both doctors agreed that I should start taking cortisone again, in the hope that the drug would slow down the progress of the disease. With time they hoped, researchers might discover a cure. Dr. Marvin encouraged us to give money to research while the specialist insisted on my doing some daily exercise so as not to lose muscle tone. They both clearly explained that the cortisone could not cure my disease but might possibly retard its growth.

My parents felt desperate. My father hired a young medical student to research my disease and see if there were any developments that my doctors were not aware of. I, not knowing the extent of my problem, didn't take it too seriously and kept reading about Edgar Cayce.

One case history really moved me. Cayce had been called in on a case by the parents of a young girl declared insane by her doctors. When the doctors suggested that she be committed to a sanitarium, her parents, unwilling to accept this fate, contacted Cayce. From a trance state Cayce described the girl's problem. He claimed that she had a wisdom tooth impinging on a nerve; if the tooth was extracted, the girl would return to normal. The result showed that he was correct. The wisdom tooth was removed and the girl resumed her normal life.

My first reaction after reading this was to feel sorry for myself that Edgar Cayce was no longer alive and couldn't be brought in to consult on my case. Then, a few nights later while milling all of this around in my mind, I discovered Steve looking despondent. It wasn't like him to be down. "They have nothing to help you with," he said. "This time it's really bad and your parents aren't telling you everything. I'm really worried," he said. "You have to do something! This thing is fatal. Don't you understand? You have to do something!" For the first time the full realization of what was happening hit me. I knew that Steve was right. I couldn't just sit back and accept this fate. If there was a way out of sickness, I had to find it, no matter where it led me.

My mind began to race as I analyzed all the material I had been reading. I reasoned that Cayce saw the wisdom tooth pressing on the nerve in the girl's brain. That meant that in the trance state part of Cayce was able to see into the girl's mouth. Part of Cayce must be mobile! His physical body was obviously not mobile while he was sleeping, so there must be a portion of him that was not physical and could see and travel beyond physical barriers. Then, seemingly from out of nowhere, came the memory of Keith Gonsalves telling me about the man in the sanctuary. I reasoned that if Cayce could do what he did, then maybe the stories Keith had told me had a basis in reality. Maybe energy could travel transatlantically—maybe it just could! At this point, with no particular conviction, but with a far more open mind than I had at eighteen, I decided to pursue my father's friend, to search for the man in the sanctuary.

- 5 -

The Commencement of Healing— My Miraculous Recovery

Fortunately we were able to contact Keith right away. He researched the matter and told us the man's name was Harry Edwards, and his sanctuary was located in Guildford, Surrey, England.

My father, who had an office in London at the time, asked one of his secretaries to call the sanctuary. We were told that I should write a letter to Mr. Edwards stating my name, address, age, and problem. It was not necessary for me to go into great detail about my illness, but I should be sure to give the name of any diagnosis made, and to make mention of whatever symptoms I was suffering from. I remember thinking that it couldn't be possible that a mere letter was all that was required of me. No one was asking me to take off my clothes, have my blood tested, or even take an X ray. Surely if this could work, it was the kindest thing, but how could it work? As I sat on my parents' poolside patio to write what became a ten-page letter, I was curious and hopeful, but quite skeptical at the same time.

My father was scheduled to make a trip to London at the end of the week. Although he didn't believe in spiritual healing, he offered to take the letter to Mr. Edwards himself.

My father saw Mr. Edwards on the morning of June 17, 1971. That evening, prior to his return, I had so much energy that I was flying! I remember that night so clearly. I went with Steve to his parents' home. For the first time in six months I didn't feel the need to drop into the first available chair. Instead I walked around, telling everyone

54

how much better I was feeling. What was even more intriguing was the sensation of pins and needles on my right side, within and surrounding the area where the biopsy had been done. I felt certain that something was happening, for I clearly felt more energy than I had known in six months. I had a sense of well-being as if I were (in the words Harry Edwards often used to describe it) "on top of the world."

Steve's family and my own noticed my exuberance and were glad. They found it hard, though, to accept my opinion that something was happening and looked for "rational" explanations for the way I was feeling. I, on the other hand, was excited. I knew what I was feeling, and I knew what it felt like to be weak all the time. There was the tingling sensation to consider, too. Up until then I had had no sensation in my liver. It wasn't until the biopsy was done that I had any real idea of where the liver was even located. Now I was feeling it tingle with energy. I remembered what Keith had told me about his friends in the Bahamas, and how they experienced a tingling sensation in their bodies before their arthritis cleared up.

When my father returned a day later, he handed me two books that Harry had given him. I began to read them immediately, devouring every word, trying to understand what healing was about and what had happened to me the other night. Surely I could not forget the feeling of energy that pervaded my being! Although the next day the tingling had ceased, and I was not experiencing that same high level of energy, I felt substantially better than I had been feeling.

About five days later I received my first letter from Harry Edwards. I have saved it all these years. It is dated June 17, 1971.

Dear Sheri Perl,

I have seen your father this morning and he has given me your letter. I am placing you within my immediate healing intercessions as from today, primarily in the first instance, to give you new strength and vitality to build up your general health, tone and resistance. This will enable the healing to overcome the hepatitis conditions—which, being a functional disorder, will need some time to be adjusted and overcome the weakness.

Your letter is very clear and the detail you provide gives me a very clear picture of your trouble.

Furthermore, the talk I have had with your father this morning, also has given me a still clearer picture of yourself; and this is so helpful to enable our intercessions to be directive and have purpose.

While it is not within my province, to give you any undertaking or promise in advance, I shall not fail to seek help to reach you in every way which can possibly be.

At the outset, I would like you to write to me weekly, giving me just a brief report of your condition, whether you are feeling stronger, happier, better, with less pain, and easier function—or not—just as it is.

I am enclosing my Notes of Absent Healing. I have given your father a copy of these; in order to explain a little about what "absent healing" entails.

I am also posting to you by sea mail a copy of our *Spiritual Healer* magazine, for your interest.

Looking forward to the future, and having good news from you,

I am,

Yours sincerely, Harry Edwards

I read the letter many times, going over and over his words in my mind. He could offer no promise in advance but he would not fail to seek help for me. It seemed so mysterious. What kind of help did he mean, and how could it find me? If it hadn't been for the improvement I was experiencing, I might think he was deluded. It really did seem, though, that something very powerful was affecting me. Something I certainly couldn't see, feel, or touch.

Two weeks after the day my father met Harry, I had my usual monthly set of blood tests. Dr. Marvin said that they were "dramatically improved." They had moved one third of the way toward normal. The doctor sounded surprised. I was ecstatic. I immediately sent off a letter to Harry to tell him the good news and became more seriously involved with my reading.

I should mention here that I was still taking cortisone

because I was afraid to diverge from my doctor's orders. Although there are those who say that healing cannot take place as long as one takes destructive drugs, Harry never asked me to change the medical course I was on.

I grew more and more fascinated with healing. To me it seemed as if magic was becoming real, or perhaps what one thought of as magic wasn't really magic at all, but rather forces and energies we didn't understand.

According to Harry, he was working in conjunction with what he referred to as "spirit doctors." He explained that when a person died his or her spirit would continue to live on in a spirit world in which there are many options for action. The spirits who take pleasure in helping to heal the sick on the earth plane are the ones he referred to as spirit doctors. Harry believed that during a period of meditation (which he referred to as his intercessions) he would reach a state of attunement in which he could communicate with spirit doctors. He would inform the spirit doctors of who needed healing, where they lived, and what the trouble seemed to be. He felt that the remainder of the healing was carried out by the spirit doctors.

Because there is no physical distance in the spirit world, a spirit can be anywhere on earth at any time. Harry taught that in many cases the spirit doctors would approach their patients while they were sleeping and their minds were more open. The spirit doctors would then direct energy to the portion of the body that was sick. They would also look beyond the physical symptom to its cause.

Harry contended that all illness has a psychosomatic origin. The cause of all illness is within the patient's mind and emotions. This does not mean that the illness is not real. It means that its cause is not physical. Harry explained that the spirit doctors try to soothe the emotional strains that give rise to the type of energy that leads to physical breakdowns. Harry felt that frustration, disappointment, or sadness could easily impair the functioning of the body. Therefore, if healing energy is directed to the dis-ease that is underlying the disease, the potential exists to cure anything, even diseases considered medically incurable.

It all sounded unbelievable, but I couldn't deny the marvelous improvement in my health. I began looking behind and within things for the evidence of spirit life, disappointed that I could not see even one apparition. If spirits were trying to help me, I wanted to see them. I realize now that, at the same time, I was far too frightened to allow my perceptions to open up to such an event.

I began to live and to breathe and to talk healing. I was so amazed by what was happening to me that I couldn't contain my excitement. I spoke to anyone who would listen. Friends with a mere common cold received the entire rundown. I had hoped to find someone who shared my enthusiasm. Reluctantly I came to see that the people I knew in 1971 weren't even remotely ready to open their minds to the idea of an unseen reality that existed in cooperation with our own. To my own mind it did not sound particularly rational either, yet beyond rationality I had my experience to consider. My experience and senses told me that something miraculous was taking place. The phenomenon of spiritual healing was still confusing to me, but its effects were not. I felt better than I had felt in a very long time. I was encouraged and hopeful that the healing would continue to reach me until I could clearly say that I was a hundred percent well again!

In the fall of 1971 Steve and I moved to Cambridge, Massachusetts, where he would be attending Harvard Business School. We found a wonderful furnished apartment with a big sunny kitchen just a short distance from school. I enrolled in the Cambridge Center for Adult Education, signing up for courses in jewelry making and Yoga breathing. I hoped that my health would continue to improve and then everything would be okay.

In September I had another set of blood tests. Dr. Marvin again reported dramatic improvement. The tests had now moved about two-thirds of the way toward normal. I was on my way, as far as I was concerned, and nothing could stop me now.

I wrote to Harry about twice a month, for myself as well as for others. I began to make an experiment of writing for people who were in difficulty and observing the results of Harry's efforts. In some cases I observed undeniably positive results, while in others I wasn't sure. I began to wonder why some people responded to Harry's efforts, as I did, with a rapid and powerful reaction, while others did not seem to be touched. Why would what worked so beautifully for one not necessarily work for another? I had read that sometimes a patient isn't "open" to the healing, but at the time I couldn't understand what that meant. Certainly, I thought, everyone wants to get well. It made no sense to me to assume that someone might be blocking the healing somehow, and so the question remained unsolved for me for quite a few years.

Probably the most valuable thing I derived from the fall in Cambridge was my Yoga breathing class. I had never realized how shallow my breathing was, nor had it ever occurred to me that the cells of my body just might need more oxygen than they were getting. Harry had sent me information on what he called "characterized breathing" (this will be outlined in Part III of this book), a deep-breathing process that he felt allowed one to absorb cosmic energy from the atmosphere. Although I tried to use it, until I took the Yoga breathing classes my habitual breathing patterns were too shallow. Now for the first time in my life I was learning to exhale deeply, completely emptying my lungs, which allowed for a far greater intake of oxygen than my body had ever known. Somehow my mind drew the analogy that now I was breathing an entire sentence, where before I was only breathing a few words. Shortly after this new breathing became habitual, I found that at about three or four o'clock each day I would feel very out of breath and would retire to my bed and pant for about an hour. It was as if the beginning of proper breathing made apparent how starved I had been for breath. As the winter approached, I was feeling stronger and more convinced that spiritual healing was a real phenomenon, despite anyone else's disbelief in it, or in me.

As December rolled around it was arranged for me to have another set of blood tests done by the liver specialist who had done the biopsy. I remember being very annoyed that he would not allow Steve to remain in the room with me while he examined me in front of a crew of interns. At least examinations for liver problems are not as embarrassing as examinations for bowel problems.

I told the doctor that I felt I was getting better. He told

me not to get my hopes up, because my disease was not curable. The cortisone I was taking could give me a false impression of having energy. I didn't dare tell him about Harry Edwards and the spirit doctors; however, I did tell him a little about the natural foods I was eating. He replied that I should be careful that I didn't turn orange from drinking too much carrot juice. It was apparent that he wasn't too impressed with my ideas and so I quickly curtailed the conversation, gave him his five vials of blood, and split. The results would be back in a week. I would call him then.

I was very anxious about the tests. If everything was proceeding as I hoped it was, then I should be pretty near normal. Along with that, I now felt that there was even more than my health at stake. Not only did I want to be well for the sake of finally being well, but I was now beginning to believe in an unseen world, and I couldn't bear to have that vision shattered. All of a sudden life had become full of magical possibilities that I did not want to lose.

I was so nervous on the Friday afternoon that I was due to call the doctor that Steve made the call for me. As he held the phone to his ear, I searched his face for a sign. When he grinned and put his thumbs up, I grabbed the phone. "Count your blessings," the doctor said. "It's really a miracle. Your tests are practically normal. It looks like the cortisone did the trick!" "The cortisone, my ass," I thought as I thanked him and put down the receiver.

That night I sat down to write to Harry. I had not yet completed my letter when, the next day, I discovered a letter from Harry waiting in my mailbox. I wish I still had it so I could repeat it word for word, but you will have to go by my memory, which about this particular letter is very, very clear. It was dated December 1971.

Dear Friend,

I feel that the healing has finally reached you. This week you will be having tests and those tests will prove to you the good news that healing has taken place.

And when you receive this news, would you please write to me so that we may all confirm the good news that healing has taken place.

My best wishes,

Harry Edwards

You can imagine my elation. As far as I was concerned, I now had conclusive proof that Harry and I were involved in some kind of paranormal communication. He not only knew about the tests without my (or anyone else) telling him, but he knew that the results were positive before I did. Surely on some metaphysical plane, it was established that I was well, and Harry could see that. I jumped up and down for joy! No one was going to tell me that it was all in my head again—or at least I wasn't going to feel threatened if they did!

On Monday I called back the specialist to tell him that I knew that I was well, and that I wanted to start getting off the cortisone right away. It had severe side effects, particularly depression. His reaction was as follows: "Young lady, if you get off the cortisone there is a fifty–fifty chance you will relapse, and if you relapse, an eighty percent chance that will you die!" He was quite clear, and I knew, as I hung up the phone, that I had an important decision to make. "He knows nothing of spiritual healing," I thought, "so how can I let him be the authority?" My decision was made. I was going to get off the drug.

I knew that my parents could not bear the knowledge of what I was going to do, so I kept it a secret from everyone but Steve.

This worked out beautifully. Steve had dropped out of school. We were both feeling disillusioned with the established world. My father had arranged for us to live and work in Utah, on a horse ranch owned by one of his friends. The plan was for Steve to work closely with the trainer of the ranch and learn as much as he could about the quarter-horse business. Eventually we would establish our own ranch in New York State, with my father as our partner.

What this meant for the present was that Steve and I were going to purchase a travel trailer, stock it with whatever we needed, and head west to St. George, Utah. As I look back,

I really have to thank my father for arranging this situation for me; it was certainly what I needed most, at this point in my recovery.

First of all, the physical separation from my family was necessary in order for me to get off cortisone. Because the withdrawal process from cortisone induces noticeable weakness, I would never be able to hide what I was doing from my parents. I knew that I could not handle their fears on top of my own.

Second, I was relieving myself of enormous mental and social pressures. If I was going to live on a ranch, I wouldn't have to burden myself with thoughts about whether I should be in college. I could let go of my concerns regarding my appearance or sense of style. And at the same time, I could forget my ill self. I could now see myself as a well person, and the people around me wouldn't know otherwise. The idea of being on my own again restored my faith that I would indeed have my own life and be able, as well, to live it.

I was relieved the day we finally left, eager to start reducing the drug. From my past experience with cortisone withdrawal, I knew that I was bound to feel very weak physically and emotionally. And because the main symptom of my last disease was weakness, I knew the withdrawal would be all the more frightening. I wouldn't know until the entire ordeal was over weather the weakness I experienced was a result of the withdrawal process or an indication of a relapse.

It's a good thing that I was prepared for a tumultuous time, for most assuredly, I had one. It doesn't sound like it would produce such dramatic results. I merely took five and a half pills instead of six upon arising and repeated that dosage twice a day. By that evening, however, I felt exhausted, and I was worried and upset. Maybe I had done the wrong thing, maybe I was really deluded. Maybe all this Harry Edwards business was in my mind and now I would relapse and die. My fears had a field day.

I then reminded myself that I was going through withdrawal and would naturally assume the worst. Usually at this point I would reread Harry's letters, focusing on the one in which he said I would be having tests soon, and that the tests would prove that healing had taken place. I tried to assure myself that some kind of healing, something I obviously didn't really understand or know if I fully believed, had taken place. I was over the disease, and just going through cortisone withdrawal. I spent many a night reading through Harry's letters, assuring myself that in fact I was well, and had not harmed myself by reducing the drug.

The withdrawal period usually lasted two to three days, during which time I felt terribly weak and ill at ease. Then my body would adjust to the present dosage and I would feel normal again. I would then wait about a week before reducing the amount so that I could prolong my experience of having energy, in this way reassuring myself that I could safely continue on this course. When I felt sufficiently confident, I would eliminate another half pill and begin the process all over again.

From my understanding of it, cortisone is normally produced in the adrenal glands and is, in actuality, a form of adrenaline, which supplies the body with energy. When cortisone is taken in large amounts, the adrenal glands register so much extra adrenaline in the body that they no longer work to produce it, and can shrink to the size of a pea. They can regenerate (thank goodness), but before they do, they have to experience the lack of cortisone in the body, and then respond to it, by producing the necessary adrenaline. That time of deficiency is the hard part.

Things were worst when I reduced the dosage from one pill to a half. We were already in Utah now, becoming close friends with Max, the horse trainer, and his wonderful family. No one could understand why I had become so quiet and withdrawn. I spent evenings in the trailer rereading Harry's letters, trying to assure myself that the severe weakness and depression would pass, When I finally adjusted to the half pill, I felt great and decided to give myself a few weeks' rest before taking the last and final plunge.

Originally I had planned to keep all of this secret from my parents until I was off the drug completely for at least two weeks, but in my elation I let it slip out. During a phone conversation, my mother asked if I needed my prescription refilled. Unable to resist, I said, "I don't need any more of the crap!"

"What did you say?" she inquired.

I boasted proudly, "I've been on a half a pill for three weeks and I feel great. Tomorrow I go to zero!"

My mother didn't know how to react. She was delighted and worried at the same time. To think that I was off the drug and feeling well was a miracle, but was it safe to be off the drug? She felt somewhat reassured to know that this had been going on for close to three months now, that I had gone through major withdrawals and had come through them feeling well. And I think she was glad that I hadn't told her earlier.

When I dropped the last half pill from my life, I expected a fairly rough time. I was thrilled to discover that I felt nothing at all. I guess the dosage, so minimal at this point, was not enough to be missed. After three days with no reaction I knew I had been freed of affliction. I wasn't fully convinced that I understood how, but I was desperate to learn and to somehow become involved in it. For the first time in many years I felt truly well. I used to take long walks around the ranch, crying with joy, from the simple feeling of nothing being wrong.

Now that I was off all medication, I decided that I would never have anything to do with medical doctors again, if I could help it. I knew that this meant that I would never have the opportunity to reverse the ileostomy, but at this time, I couldn't imagine that I would ever be able to make the choice to put myself through surgery. I was so grateful to be alive and well that I figured the ileostomy was one cross I would have to bear.

I was full of wonder and gratitude. Gratitude at being alive, and wonder at the forces that enabled me to be so.

Part II

- 6 -

My First Conclusions Regarding My Healing

As a result of my astonishing recovery and the means through which it came about, I was drawn to study the inner world and the powers and forces therein. After all, my body had become well very quickly in what seemed to me direct response to the efforts of Harry Edwards in England. Somehow he had reached me, and had done so through a means that was obviously not physical. No physical contact was made, no physical medicine was taken, nothing in the outside physical world had changed, and yet the most dramatic changes had taken place in my body.

As I began to sort out the events as I saw them, certain conclusions came to mind: Harry, through thought or meditation or—in his words—attunement, was able to direct energy to me. In response to this energy, illness in my body was overcome.

Because I could not see, feel, hear, touch, or taste this energy, I concluded that the energy was not physical. Because its effects were quite physical, I could not deny its presence. I therefore concluded that energy, not perceivable to the average human being exists, similar to the way that television and radio waves exist in the atmosphere. I began to think of this energy as spiritual waves; henceforth I could now accept the term *spiritual energy*, for it meant just that: energy that existed, but not in physical form.

Because physical form can be so drastically affected by this energy, it is obviously receptive to it. Because it is receptive to it there must be a counterpart within the physi-

67

cal system that allows for this acceptance. Since we do not
know of any part of the physical body that allows for the
acceptance of spiritual energy, the receptacle of this energy
must be nonphysical itself, or spirit. I now could accept that
I must be in part spirit; and that all beings must be in part
spirit. Somehow the spiritual essence of all life must be
embedded in it from the start, but I had never bothered to
think about it, and had always assumed that what I saw was
all that existed. I now began to think that what I saw was
just the outermost covering of a much greater reality of
spirit, which interpenetrated all that I saw. Not only did it
interpenetrate it, but in actuality it might just govern it, for
the spiritual energy was able to heal from the inside that
which was not considered healable from the outside.

It began to seem to me that life worked from the inside
out, and that many forces that we might not be in touch
with could have a controlling effect on our lives. If this was
true, it seemed clear to me that I had better try to learn
what those forces were and how they worked in me, or I
might just end up ill again. Therefore, I consciously began
my quest for a greater understanding of what seemed to me
a very mysterious spirit world.

I spent a lot of time reading books about healing. I was
fascinated with the concept of a spirit reality that not only
existed but worked in cooperation with our own. I wanted
to be in touch with this reality, and longed for experiences
that would prove to me even more conclusively that spirit
existence was real. Despite my experience, I still had my
doubts, which I desired to eliminate.

To this end I organized all sorts of spiritual meetings,
holding seances (unsuccessfully, I might add) with anyone
who would take part, including many of the ranch hands,
who neither believed nor cared for any of my ideas. I tried
to develop my own healing abilities by working on the ill
animals at the ranch, placing my hands on them and imagin-
ing that healing energy was entering into them. You could
say that my focus was turned inward, as I tried to experience and understand the spiritual nature of life, but at the
same time I was learning an enormous amount about living
on the land: cooking, sewing, and tending to animals. As
Steve worked with Max, the horse trainer of the ranch, I

had the opportunity to spend a good deal of time with his wife. I grew to love Yvonne, and their seven children, feeling a part of their healthy, loving, strong, hardworking family. My environment was challenging without being at all threatening.

After a year in the west, Steve and I drove our travel trailer to upstate New York, where we searched for and found our farm. I had a very strong feeling about one particular farm, and felt that it was meant to be ours. I also sensed that when we finally settled onto it, I would find a teacher who would teach me what I was seeking to know.

Prior to settling on our farm, Steve and I made a trip to England to meet Harry Edwards, something that was very important to me. We both knew that once we began to work our farm, we would be responsible for the lives of many animals and would not be able to get away so easily.

I found Harry to be the same down-to-earth, kind, and good-natured man that he was in his letters. In his simple and easy manner, he showed us around the beautiful grounds and gardens of Burrows Lea, and then took us inside to join in a healing session. I anticipated feeling something momentous, and was disappointed not to feel intense heat or energy emanating from his hands. I was still looking for tangible proof of spirit reality.

While roaming the grounds around the sanctuary, we met a young man from Ireland who said that he was a medium. Peter was very helpful to me and satisfied much of my curiosity about the spiritual plane. We spoke much over the next several days.

Before we parted, Peter gave me a list of British books he thought would be helpful to me. Among them were books by White Eagle, a spirit communicator who spoke through a medium by the name of Grace Cooke. The material was fascinating and more important to me than the psychology books that had been my fancy a few years before.

I liked White Eagle immediately. I felt that he was a very loving spirit and his writings further confirmed my views that realities, beyond those we can see, feel, and touch, do indeed exist. When he spoke of healing, he expressed the need for meditation as a way of tuning yourself into a higher vibration. I remembered that Harry had said that it was necessary for him to reach a state of attunement in order to make contact with the spirit doctors. As I thought about it, I began to realize that practically everything I had read concerning healing mentioned meditation.

I decided that the time had come for me to learn to meditate. Not knowing how else to begin, I drove into town from the farm one day and purchased a number of books. None was helpful. Reading about meditation didn't exactly help me learn how to do it. I understood in theory that meditation involved focusing on one thought, word, or image in order to slow down the thoughts rushing through your mind. In practice, I had no idea where to begin.

I was considering Transcendental Meditation when a friend of mine who had recently completed TM came to the farm. I told her of my desire to meditate and she offered to teach me about TM. She also chose a mantra for me.

Cynthia explained that in TM you are given a mantra by your instructor. A mantra is a word or sound that you repeat over and over again in your head, focusing your attention upon it and away from your usual thoughts. Cynthia chose for me the word *sohom*. She said that it meant mother, and described the way she was viewing me then, as an earth mother, surrounded by my growing animals and plants. I was delighted with her choice and together we set up a special room in the upstairs of my home to be used as a meditation room.

We cut fresh flowers and placed them around the room, lit candles, and set incense to burn (something I still love to do) before we sat down to meditate. I don't know exactly what I expected, but I was definitely disappointed. I said the word *sohom* over and over in my mind but it seemed impossible to keep my mind from wandering. I had remembered reading that it was natural for the mind to wander. It was advised that in this situation one should, without getting upset, take notice of it, and then center oneself again on the mantra. I tried but I couldn't help getting upset, and when I resumed focusing on my mantra, I didn't feel centered. I just felt as if I were repeating a boring and monotonous word. I had hoped to reach attunement and meet the gods, and all I was doing was repeating some dumb word. But I knew that instant success might not be attainable and that I would have to keep at it a little longer before forming an opinion.

As a result of my interest in meditation, I began reading books about Eastern philosophy. Again I read about transcending the ego through meditation. I found myself intrigued because it seemed that my life could be painless if I wasn't suffering from disappointments and desires. Even the sadness of my ileostomy would be lessened if my ego wasn't so powerful. It also seemed that I might be more able to maintain a state of positive thinking (something Harry Edwards and White Eagle felt extremely necessary) if I had less of an ego to satisfy. Wasn't it my ego that found fault with my life and with myself? I also understood through my reading that when one truly transcended one's ego, one was then able to fully merge with the greater forces of the universe, enabling one to become a more powerful person, or even a healer. All of this appealed to me. I committed myself to daily meditation to see what would develop.

Ever since the ileostomy I had taken a bath each morning in order to totally remove the appliance from my body and cleanse myself in the warm, comforting water. During this time I would dilate the stoma, as I still had a constriction problem. Because this usually took about thirty minutes, I decided to meditate while soaking in the tub so as not to take any longer getting my day started.

What began as a matter of practicality became a matter of practice when I discovered that meditation and bathing worked extremely well together. The warm water helps to induce relaxation, and being in the bath removes you from the rest of your home and activities.

Every morning I would immerse myself in a warm tub, make myself as comfortable as possible, dilate the stoma, and begin to repeat the sound *sohom*. For a while nothing at all interesting happened. Then about two weeks later I began to notice how much deeper my breathing had become and how relaxed my arms and legs were. Sometime after that, while concentrating on the sound *sohom*, I began to hear my own breath. As I listened further, the sound of my breath seemed to speak the sound *sohom*. It sounded to me as if my breath said *so* as I inhaled and *hom* as I exhaled. At times I could just forget about thinking the word altogether and listen instead to the sound of my breath. *Sohom, sohom* would repeat over and over as I breathed in and out.

I found that this did calm me down and put me in a better frame of mind, but as far as overcoming my ego and merging with higher forces, I seemed to be getting nowhere. I was still ruled by my desires, while my ego remained relentless. I wanted to develop as a healer and I longed to grow spiritually, but I found it hard to love everyone unconditionally, or to feel only happy emotions, or think only pleasant thoughts. Everything I read spoke of finding peace through transcending common human foibles, and yet I was human and felt locked into my humanity. I became very frustrated.

My dream was to travel to England and study with Harry Edwards himself. Of course I knew this wasn't possible, and Harry wasn't teaching any classes for healers anyway. I was thrilled when Harry sent me literature about a correspondence course he was developing to train healers. For the first time in my life I was thoroughly enthusiastic about the idea of studying. I read the textbooks, studied Harry's theories with zest and determination, and was more than eager to take the written examination that arrived a few months later. I was not surprised when I passed. I was also extremely happy to discover that as a result, I was certified as a member of the National Fellowship of Healing. This certification came through the National Federation of Spiritual Healers, of which Harry was the honorary president.

I also continued my efforts to learn more about meditation. I attended classes and consulted gurus. Each time I left a session, however, I felt definite disappointment. I was no more enlightened than when I entered the session. My instructors basically confirmed that the technique I was already using was more than adequate. At any rate, I was proud that I had discovered the right technique on my own. This realization gave me greater faith in my own instincts and inclinations.

It was now clear to me that I had no idea of what truth or enlightenment or oneness with the universe meant. They sounded like desirable states but it seemed to me that neither I, nor most of the people who talked about them, really understood what they were talking about. I didn't know if I could ever be in complete agreement with everything in the

universe. I didn't have any idea what it was that I was trying
to achieve. I continued meditation in the hope that it would
help bring me closer to where I wanted to be—although I
couldn't define what or where that was. I sensed a feeling of
mental freedom inside me that longed to be unleashed. I
sensed a state of greater peace of mind inside me that I
longed to tap. I sensed things, but I couldn't put my finger
on them. I hoped that meditation would help me to find
them.

Then one day I overheard a young woman speaking to
another woman at a meditation meeting. The first one asked,
"What do you do about desire, when you find yourself
overcome by it?" The other answered, "I meditate it away.
I meditate on the light and it all disappears. The light
dissolves it." "Nonsense," I thought. It was right then and
there that something inside of me snapped.

I sensed that there was inherent value in meditating, and I
knew that I would continue to do so. However, I was tired
of theories that suggested that I become desireless and egoless.
Were the full range of human emotions supposed to be
squashed down into some blissful benignness that I'll admit
sounded lovely, but just might not be real? After all we are
human. We are endowed with all kinds of feelings and
emotions. We desire our first breath, and so we breathe.
We desire to be, and so we live. How could all desire be
wrong?

I grew very confused. I wanted to be a healer, but I knew
that I could not become all those lily-white things that my
books and instructors required. My emotions, my desires,
my unique personal self were with me no matter how deeply
I explored meditation. I felt that I could not give myself up
in order to find a deeper self. I realized that my longing to
be a healer sprang largely from my desire to help others, not
an emotion that one would want to squelch.

I began trying to separate the contents of the meditation
package. I wanted to continue to meditate for various reasons but not to stamp out my ego, or to eliminate desire, or
to transcend the human condition. What I did want to do
was gain some control over my own negativity and emotions.

During meditation, many negative, fearful and unhappy
thoughts filled my mind, thoughts I seemed to have very

little control over. I became aware of ingrained patterns of thinking. Fearful thoughts, angry thoughts, stress-provoking thought were not uncommon visitors to my mind.

Although meditation was relaxing, it did not help me change these thoughts. I became increasingly aware of my thoughts, but I had no idea how to change them. I realized that my fears and negative thoughts blocked me from the peace of mind I so desperately desired. How, I wondered, does one change one's way of thinking?

I was longing for help and direction on that fateful day when I discovered the teacher who would finally help me sort all of this out. The person whose presence I sensed when Steve and I first came east to purchase our farm was about to enter my life.

- 7 -

Enter Seth and the Discovery of My Personal Beliefs; A Fuller Understanding of the Causes Behind My Illness

I first learned of Jane Roberts through one of my sister's friends. Alfredo, who was deeply involved with Jane's work, insisted that Sondra tell me about an incredible medium who lived in the town of Elmira, a twenty-five minute car ride from my farm. This medium, he claimed, was responsible for bringing through a personality of great wisdom. This personality, called Seth, was writing books through Jane—books that were changing the lives of many people.

I was immediately drawn to Jane and Seth. I wasted no time in heading for the Elmira bookstore to purchase all of the Seth books available.

Fortunately the man in the bookstore seemed to have a good deal of practical information concerning Jane. He looked up her number in the telephone book for me and told me that she was listed under her husband's name, Butts. That explained why I couldn't find a number for any Jane Roberts in Elmira. He also informed me that she held weekly ESP classes in her home, the very idea of which sent waves of excitement throughout my body. "Maybe this is it," I thought. "Maybe I'm about to become involved with the teacher I've been waiting for all along."

As I drove back to the farm I planned in my mind how I would call Jane and express to her my need to be a member of her class. I hadn't even read one word in her books, yet I felt a tremendous longing to learn from her.

When Jane answered the phone she sounded warm and friendly. I told her that I had been very interested in spiritual healing and mediumship for a long time. I expressed my strong desire to attend her ESP class. She asked me if I had read any of her books. I told her that I had just purchased a few of them that day. She explained to me that the prerequisite for joining her class was to read *The Seth Material* and *Seth Speaks*. At the time both books were sitting in my lap. If I could have gobbled them up that instant, I would have. Instead I promised her that I would start reading immediately. Jane told me to call her again once I had completed the books.

Now I have never been a fast reader and those of you who have read Seth know that the material isn't particularly fast reading. I was working my way through the books when I felt that I could wait no longer. I called Jane again approximately one month later. When asked if I had finished the books I told Jane "not completely." I crossed my fingers and made a silent wish. Jane hesitated a moment and then graciously said that I could attend the next class.

My excitement was enormous. I had read in the books that Seth came through Jane during these ESP classes and actually talked to the students. I have to admit that I was terrified at the idea of Seth speaking directly to me, but I wanted to experience the phenomenon anyway. So far my experience with mediumship was limited to reading, looking at photographs taken at seances, and listening to tapes. All of this I had found very interesting. I knew, however, that it could not compare to being there. I also had a very strong sense that I would make valuable friends through these classes, friends that would last throughout my life.

Because of my hurry, my conscious understanding of the Seth books was shallow. On the night of my first class, most of the discussion went right over my head.

Class was always held on Tuesdays at eight P.M. As I entered Jane and Rob's crowded living room I was shocked to see people drinking wine, smoking cigarettes, cracking jokes, and acting, it seemed to me, in a manner that was very unspiritual.

One couch seemed filled with as many people as could fit

on it. All the available chairs were taken while people crowded between, in front of, and behind the chairs.

Not knowing anyone and feeling shy, I took a seat on the floor in a corner of the room and watched. Everyone seemed well acquainted; animated conversations sprang up in every direction. Occasionally I noticed another person who, like myself, sat quietly, but for the most part the group was boisterous. The age range varied. I saw many people who looked to be around my age (twenty-two), while the oldest members must have been in their eighties.

I was trying to figure out who was Jane when she took over control of the room, requesting that everyone settle down. Jane began class by asking members about their dreams. I listened, barely comprehending, as the students gladly volunteered information. Jane laughed at some of the remarks that were made and lit herself a cigarette. She was a small, thin woman with dark shoulder-length hair. Her nose was prominent, but what stood out most on her face were her dark, sharp, intelligent, intent eyes. Though small in stature, Jane didn't seem small in any other way. There was power and wit and wisdom behind those eyes. I felt immediate respect for her.

I was involved in listening to conversations going back and forth between Jane and the class members when all of a sudden I heard a loud and powerful voice take over the conversation. All eyes were riveted on Jane as Seth removed her glasses and became the focal point of the room. "Good evening," Seth said, and "good evening" some answered. I felt frozen to my spot on the floor. I was so scared that I couldn't imagine how the class members interacted so casually with Seth. As I looked at Jane and studied her she definitely appeared different: more masculine, stronger, even more powerful. Although I was too overwhelmed to understand Seth's words there was no doubt in my mind of his presence within Jane's body. A different energy emanated from her now.

I was greatly surprised by Seth's entry. I assumed that candle lighting, or light dimming, or meditating on Jane's part would be necessary to bring Seth through. Instead it happened as easily and naturally as switching channels on a TV set. It seemed that Seth could come and go at will, responding to the conversations that took place between the students and Jane. His voice was strong and powerful, not weak and otherworldly. He didn't seem the least bit concerned with appearing quiet or dignified, but instead went out of his way to be humorous and jovial. He teased and cajoled, raised his voice and lowered his voice, spoke strongly and emphatically as well as softly and tenderly. Although I was not concentrating on his words, there was no denying his presence and the impact it was making on me.

I lost track of the time. Midway through the evening, Jane called a class break and left the room. "Now what am I going to do?" I wondered. Because Steve and I were beginning to have marital problems, I had attended class alone. I didn't know anyone and felt intimidated by the many outspoken people. Feeling more than a little lost, I walked into the small kitchen of Jane's Water Street apartment and began to pour myself a cup of tea. I felt someone enter behind me and turned to face a tall, dark, young man. I was instantly attracted to him, and when he asked me how I was doing I felt a rush of energy between us. I said I was okay; I wondered who he was. I knew no one there who I could ask, and to make matters worse, I was married. Yet I could hardly deny my desire to know this man.

Soon class resumed and I kept my eye on that young man throughout the rest of the evening. I didn't talk at all in class except to answer Jane when she asked me what my impression of class was. "Refreshing," I said. "Refreshing to hear so many people speak honestly to each other." It was the only thing I could think of saying. Shortly after, Jane said that class was over. I approached her quickly to thank her for letting me come. Much to my surprise and pleasure, Jane said that I was welcome to attend class regularly. She added that if for some reason I was unable to attend class, I should phone.

While people milled around talking to Jane and to each other, Sue Watkins, a regular member of the class, walked over to the young man that I had my eye on. Sue told him that he reminded her of Kurt Vonnegut. He noticed me watching and we smiled briefly at each other. From that time on, in my mind, he became the Kurt Vonnegut guy. As I drove back to the farm that night, my mind was filled with thoughts of Jane and Seth, the energy of the evening, and the Kurt Vonnegut guy. Although I didn't speak to him again for several years, I thought of him. He symbolized to me the man that I was looking for. When faced with the dissatisfactions of my marriage, I thought of the Kurt Vonnegut guy and wondered if I would ever be given a second chance to fall in love.

When my second Seth class rolled around, Steve said that he wanted to attend with me. Jane said that if I was comfortable with that, it was certainly okay with her. She knew that he hadn't come with me the first time and I had indicated some marital problems. But Steve and I were trying to sweep them under the rug again, not knowing what other course to take.

Sometimes avoidance worked for a while, but eventually the same issues would arise. I would grow dissatisfied with who Steve was and would always want him to think and act differently. He would always become frustrated with my lack of interest in fulfilling his needs.

In part, we both knew that I felt paralyzed sexually due to my ileostomy. I felt much more comfortable with my clothes on than off. Steve had hoped that time would eventually bring me out of my shell. Instead, I had less and less interest in sex as time went on.

I was very confused. I knew that I longed for so much outside of my little world but I felt that I dare not reach for it. I felt safe and secure with Steve and yet unfulfilled.

At my third Seth class Jane was talking about Harry Edwards as I entered the room. "I've had an experience with Harry Edwards," I eagerly said. "Tell us about it," Jane responded. Before I knew it, all the eyes in the room were focused on me. I became nervous. My lips seemed stuck together as I began to explain how Harry Edwards cured me of liver disease. I explained the amazing blood-test results. Before I could finish my story it seemed as if twenty people shouted all at once, "What beliefs did you change? You must have changed some beliefs. What were they?"

I knew I was in trouble now. "Uh, beliefs, I didn't change any," I said. "It just happened."

"Impossible," the crowd shouted. "You had to have changed some beliefs, or it couldn't have happened!"

"My God," I thought, "what is a belief and what are they all talking about?"

The class members were waiting for my response, and I felt unable to find one. Jane, who I'm certain noticed my discomfort, explained that sometimes we change beliefs without even realizing it. I was off the hook. I still didn't understand what they were talking about, however, and I decided to be very quiet so as not to make a fool of myself in front of this boisterous and overwhelming bunch.

As a teacher of *The Seth Material*, I have always recommended that people read the third Seth book, *The Nature of Personal Reality* first because that book finally saved me from my confusion. To me *NOPR* (short for *Nature of Personal Reality*) is the handbook of all the Seth books. It is about the nature of our personal realities, how we form our own experience through our thoughts and beliefs, and how we can change our own experience through changing our thoughts and beliefs.

Without trying to rewrite a Seth book (which I could never do; I am no match for Seth's genius), I would like to outline briefly some of Seth's ideas and look at how they applied to my life.

According to Seth, we form our own experience. We are responsible for what happens to us. If we are hit by disaster, we did something to bring it about. In other words, we are not victims.

It is not as if someone says, "Hey, I want to be hit by a car today or become seriously ill." It is not usually a conscious decision. The event is nonetheless formed by the energy of the recipient.

Your energy goes out from you and shapes the reality that you know. The kind of energy you give off is a result of your beliefs. Your beliefs are your thoughts backed up by your emotions. We all have many of them. Some of our beliefs were formed in childhood. If you believe in reincarnation, then it may be that some of your beliefs were born in other lives and are still present in you today. But wherever your beliefs originated, they are now responsible for the reality you experience.

According to Seth, we create our own reality through our minds, spirits, conscious thoughts and feelings, and unconscious thoughts and feelings. We create and draw to us every aspect of our experience, and are therefore responsible for whatever happens to us.

In other words, your fortune or misfortune is not a matter of chance or good luck, but is the result of beliefs and expectations. All that you expect, imagine, and concentrate on will be faithfully molded into your experience. The difficulty, as I see it, is that so many people have no idea that their beliefs are just that, beliefs. Instead they see them as reality.

For example, people often think they are not capable of achieving a certain goal. This may or may not be true (most times it is not true), but because they believe it to be, they prevent themselves from reaching that goal, feeling then all the more certain about their belief. "You see," they often say, "I knew I could never make this work." Although they do not recognize it, their belief created the reality that they know, and nothing beyond that.

It is not difficult to determine your beliefs. If you study your own conscious thoughts, they will show you a great deal of what you believe. Everyone is constantly writing scripts in their heads. The scripts are formed by their belief systems. For example, if you imagine yourself arguing with your boss, or your mate, or your child, you probably soon will be. If you begin to pay attention to your thoughts, you can begin to make connections between what you think and believe and the reality that you experience. You can then go still further and change those thoughts and beliefs that are not giving you the results you want, thereby consciously changing your reality.

Finally understanding this myself, I now knew what the students meant when they asked what beliefs I had changed in order to become well. But I still had no idea *what* beliefs I had changed. There certainly hadn't been a conscious change, yet I recognized that at one time I believed spiritual healing was merely a figment of someone's delirium. Obviously, many beliefs had changed in me as a result of my being so sick, but I remained unaware of the process.

Although at first I couldn't understand how Seth's teachings applied to my life, I somehow felt I had stumbled onto a heap of truth, that the keys to the universe were inside us, that reality somehow worked from the inside out. As I read further in *NOPR*, I attempted to apply each and every statement to my personal life, to see which ones were true.

The more I read, the more clearly I began to see some of my personal beliefs. I still could not understand how I had created my severe illness or had chosen it, but I was astounded, as some of my present beliefs became apparent, how clearly they reflected my experience.

My first revelation was that I believed that my body was bad and undesirable as a result of the ileostomy. This was nothing new. I was aware of my feelings about my body since the surgery. The difference now was that I realized I was holding a belief that my body was bad, and that it was not necessarily reality. Maybe my body wasn't so disgusting. It did what everyone else's did, only differently. And then I began to examine further my beliefs about the human body and its biology, discovering the fact that I had never been comfortable with my body and its workings.

I can remember how uneasy I felt if I was on a date and had to excuse myself to go to the bathroom. In some mixed-up way I believed that urinating or moving one's bowels was not feminine and felt ashamed of the most necessary of bodily processes. I felt that my breasts should be placed delicately inside lace bras and my vagina neatly hidden away in lace panties. Then they were clean and feminine and pretty. The fact that they were part of something much greater and spiritual than all that nonsense completely eluded me.

In a regular ESP class, held on December 10, 1974, Seth's speaking about the human biology had a profound effect upon me. I would like to quote a small section from that session here:

You think that the soul is a white wall with nothing written upon it, and so your idea of sacrilege is to shit upon it, not realizing that the shit and the soul are one, and that the biological is spiritual, and that, again, if you will forgive my homey concept, that flowers grow from the shit of the earth. The true communion is that all things of this earth return to it and are consumed and rise up again in a new life that is never destroyed, never annihilated, though always changing form.

So when you shrink from such words or meanings, why do you shrink? Because you do not trust the biology of your being or the integrity of your soul in flesh. You are people! You are made of the stuff of the earth, and the dust from the stars has formed into the shit that lies in piles—warm piles that come from the animals and the beasts and the warm creatures of the earth, and that shit fertilizes the flowers, and the ground, and is a part of it.

How *dare* any of you, therefore, set yourselves up against that or in conflict with it?

I realized that my disgust for my ileostomy was powered by my disgust for my biological processes. I also realized that as long as I maintained the view that human-body functions were disgusting, I would always be in conflict with my life. I didn't know how to change these beliefs, but I hoped that understanding them as beliefs, as opposed to facts, would make a difference. It did. In a subtle way I felt less bad about my body.

Like magic, once I had become aware of one belief, many more began to reveal themselves to me. Once I came to see that something I had always taken for reality was merely my perception of reality, then everything was up for reevaluation. How much of what I thought was really as it was? How much was a product of my beliefs? Seth was saying that everything was a product of my beliefs, that no "rock-bed reality" existed. Instead there were many versions and perceptions, all which I could control. This concept was fascinating and allowed for all kinds of possibilities, but it was also disturbing as well.

I remember walking into writing class (a small group Jane taught during the day, which I joined far more out of a desire to be around Jane than to write) feeling shaky and unsupported. "It's as if I had my table all set," I said, "and even if the place settings were not so hot, they were there and they supported me. Now I feel that none of them are real and I therefore have to remove them, and my table is bare, and it's scary!"

"Well," Jane answered. "There is no reason why you should feel that you have to overturn everything. Keep the beliefs that work for you. Discard only what you want to discard. No one is telling you that you must turn your entire world upside down." But I felt as though my world was turning upside down of its own accord. "None of it is real," I retorted, "so how can I keep it?"

I was no longer sure if I truly knew anything. Every opinion that I held (and I held many opinions about everything) now had to be reevaluated. "This is what I believe about this," I would think, "but is it in fact true, or just my perception of it? If it is merely my perception of it, do I want to believe this anymore? Is it productive for me to believe this?" And in this manner I questioned everything.

As this process went on, I began to experience new feelings associated with the issues I was examining. As I realized, for example, that maybe my body was not so terrible and only my beliefs made me feel so bad, the pain and horror that had been locked deep inside of me rushed to the surface and demanded release. Now, for the first time, I was ready to face that pain.

I remember spending an entire weekend crying. How I longed for my once perfect body and the nonchalance that had accompanied it. My face dripping with tears, the source of which seemed limitless, I agonized over all the jealousy I felt toward other women who still had their bodies intact. And yet I knew this wasn't their fault. I ached for something I knew I didn't have with Steve. I had known it when I walked down the aisle, but I knew it with far more certainty now. I wondered if I would ever feel secure enough to go off on my own. I understood now that my belief in my own inadequacy had manipulated me into thinking that marrying Steve would be the answer to my problems. I knew now that that belief was limiting and was causing both Steve and me a lot of pain.

Every time I thought I had finished crying, another image of my body, or of a beautiful girl in a bikini, or of the Kurt Vonnegut guy would rush through my mind, bringing with it an onrush of fresh tears. I felt trapped. I knew what I wanted, but I felt it could never happen. I cried for what I desired and believed would always be denied me—a second chance at love and the reconnection of my bowel.

When I emerged from the weekend, I felt better. I knew my problems were not solved, but I felt lighter. I knew that I was not yet ready to make any dramatic changes in my life with Steve, but I felt more optimistic. I had a sense that the future would somehow lend a hand.

Seth class became the most exciting event in my life. My fear of Seth was turning into love and respect as I grew to see that he had no interest in exposing my secrets to the class. What had made me fear him so was, again, my beliefs. His wisdom and concern for each one of us forced me to confront all the ridiculous things I had projected upon him. For instance, as I saw it, underneath my exterior lived one scared, marred, hurting turkey who really wasn't what she pretended to be. I feared that Seth, seeing through my façade, would expose my secrets. That ridiculous logic was formed in my beliefs. Seth never saw any of us as anything but good and tried to impress upon each of us, time and again, the basic goodness of what we were. It was through his teachings that I came to see how little trust and respect and love I felt for my own being. In his books, and in many of the classes, Seth spoke to us of the worth and imperfect perfection of our beings right now.

And yet a cat is a cat, a perfect cat, whether it is flawed or has a broken foot, or whether it can hear or not hear, or whether it is ancient or young. A cat is a perfect cat. Now you can understand that. But in the same way you have a responsibility to be yourselves as a cat has to be itself. To express the joyful creature nature that is your own. And through that expression your spirituality will flower.

As I read and listened to such statements, I was forced to take a look at myself. I knew that I didn't feel like a perfect cat. I felt marred, and yet I did recognize that when I looked at an animal with a broken leg, it didn't bother me. I just saw an animal with a broken leg, not a lesser creature. I knew now that I had a lot of beliefs to change. It seemed like a tremendous amount of work, and I didn't know where to begin. I knew this much: I had nothing better to do with my life, and if I couldn't find a way to accept my body and myself, I'd never be free to enjoy life.

One thing that I had learned from my closeness to death's door was that no one is given forever to make life work. I wanted my life to work. I didn't really know what that meant, or how I was going to do it, but I sensed that there was happiness inside of me, happiness that I could possibly tap. I felt that if there was a way to change my perception of my body, I would have to find it. And whether that led me to or away from Steve, I would find my way.

How to go about the business of changing beliefs was another matter. Seth had said that some beliefs could change automatically, as a result of recognizing them as beliefs. However, Seth never said that it would always be easy to change all of them. Each of us would have to discover our own ways, working within the laboratories of our own minds. He gave us some very useful exercises in his books, but again stressed the individual nature of any exercise. According to Seth there was no "right" way to do anything. Each of us would have to discover the ways that worked best for ourselves.

In many ways we are all like our own hypnotists and our own subjects, hypnotized by our own beliefs. Seth discussed suggestion as one possible way of changing beliefs. When questioned by a student about how to believe in his basic goodness (when he didn't believe that he was good), Seth instructed him to tell himself over and over that he was good until he believed it. Seth said that we should watch the suggestions that we were feeding ourselves, and consciously change our suggestions wherever we found them limiting.

It seemed to me that the process was threefold. Certainly you first had to recognize what your belief was. Then allow yourself to feel the emotions connected with that belief, and experience its presence in your life. If, at this point, you experienced your belief as limiting, you had to try to change it, or at least alter your perspective on it.

Because I was already working with meditation and deep breathing every morning, I decided to add some belief work. I figured that the relaxed state of meditation would make my mind more open to suggestions. I knew that it was essential that I start suggesting that my body was good, my being was good, and that there was nothing so wrong about me that I should live in fear of exposure. I could feel the enormous need to absorb these beliefs into my psyche in order to just make life bearable.

While I could clearly see how some of my present beliefs were making me suffer, I couldn't understand how I had created my illness in the first place, or why I chose such a difficult challenge for myself. It seemed to me, at the time, to have come from out of nowhere. Seth told us that nothing is ever thrust upon us from the outside but is formed on the inside first, through our thoughts and beliefs, until it is finally made physical in reality. But accepting responsibility for my suffering seemed impossible. I felt the rightness of the Seth teachings, yet it was hard for me to accept that everyone who suffered was creating their own situation. How could my power have worked so against me?

I decided that I would have to take a closer look at the years prior to my illness. Who was I as a child, what did I feel, and behind that, what did I believe?

As I began to look back, all the mystery came out of the picture and the truth was perfectly clear.

I had always been frightened as a child. I didn't realize that I was scared, I thought that everyone felt the same way I did. I existed in waves of anxiousness, experiencing that feeling referred to as "butterflies," a jumpy, nervous feeling in the pit of my stomach, on and off throughout the day.

I don't know when these fears began. I was told that the first two years of my life were draining to everyone around me, that I wailed and screamed from a bad case of colic. I joke sometimes, and call the colic the forerunner to ileitis. They certainly produce similar symptoms, and it's interesting to me that I was plagued at birth with the same kind of intestinal pain as with my first disease. If, in fact, nothing happens from the outside alone, then, at a point as early as birth, a being can possess beliefs that interfere with the smooth functioning of his or her body!

As I looked back, I couldn't blame my parents for the fear that engulfed me as a child. It seemed larger and greater than them. Although they both strove to raise me in a loving and secure environment, my feelings prevailed. Of course at the time I was basically unaware of these feelings. I lived around them because they were a part of my being. I felt frightened in many situations, and safest when my mother was in sight.

I can still remember, rather vividly, my first day at nursery school. Mother took me to Happy Hours with the hope that they would be happy hours for me. The teacher amused me with a piece of clay, figuring it would make me forget my mother, and encouraged my mother to leave. What she didn't know was that I had radar on my mother, and, when all of a sudden the clay seemed to disappear in my hands, I knew my mother was gone. Panic turned into tears, which flowed incontrollably until I knew that my mother was on her way back to the school. Only then was I willing to lie down on my Bow Wow blanket and eat a few gumdrops.

By the time I entered kindergarten I knew that I couldn't get away with being such a baby in school and began to suppress the impulse to cry. Although this wasn't always possible, and I sometimes had to bear the embarrassment of crying in class, from an early age I learned how to suppress my emotions.

Throughout my growing up, although I was not aware of what it was, I had a general fear that I projected in many different directions. For example, I would begin feeling uneasy on Sunday afternoons, dreading leaving home on Monday mornings. Because I was so tense by Monday morning, I found it impossible to eat breakfast before leaving for school.

I was uptight about the school bus. I feared that I would miss it in the mornings and be unable to find it after school. My greatest fear was that if I couldn't find it after school, I would never get back home again. Of course this was totally irrational as the buses lined up in front of the school every afternoon, waited for a least fifteen minutes after school dismissal, and sported a sign in the window marked with the number of the bus.

But at the time, this fear was bigger than life. I was nervous about tests and about the fact that I was seldom completely prepared for my classes. I was constantly distracted by my fears in class, paying little or no attention to my teachers at all as I ran through in my mind how I would get home after school, or face some other crisis.

Life for me was a series of these feelings. I took them for granted because they were such a familiar part of me. I went away to summer camp for seven summers, always going through enormous trauma about leaving home. I learned how to conceal it from everyone, including, at times, myself. Not that I didn't feel it. But I didn't think it was something that I could ever change, it was so natural to me.

Often I have thought about being taught to read and write, add and subtract, punctuate and diagram sentences, dissect frogs—the list goes on and on—but I never attended a class that dealt with who I was or what I felt. Self-examination and exploration were the furthest things from the academic curriculum, which in turn produced many intelligent yet unfulfilled people. It was clear to me that although I had learned how to act right, dress well, get through my studies, and fit in socially, my childhood consisted of one emotional trauma after another. Of course I understand that I was not the only frightened child who ever grew up in this world, and that every child who is frightened does not become ill. However, the anxiety I lived with for sixteen years prior to becoming ill, was the cause of my sickness. That anxiety, which centered in my abdomen, was the very same place where my ileitis would eventually grow. The dis-ease grew into disease. This process did not happen overnight. Long before the first symptoms of ileitis became apparent, my fear and anxiety were setting the stage for my intestines to become inflamed.

Once I saw the connection between my dis-ease and disease, I could no longer deny it, and yet it seemed less of a burden than I thought. It wasn't as if I had asked to be sick because I wanted to hurt myself. Illness was the only effect my energy could have because it had no other escape or release. Even now, if I experience a nerve-racking event, my intestines can get upset and send me more frequently to the bathroom. If I were to sustain that same kind of nervous energy again, every day of my life, I know that I would be inviting ileitis. Although I could remember my tension, and see its results in my body, I still didn't understand the beliefs that were responsible for my fear.

Then on the evening of July 12, 1975, Jane had a class. By now I knew everyone who was a regular member and noticed that there was a student there who had not been coming regularly. I thought he looked familiar. Although nine months had passed since my first Seth class, I thought he just might be the Kurt Vonnegut guy. We took notice of each other.

Then Seth came through, and I was immediately drawn into his words. "As long as you believe that you dwell in a universe that is a threat, you must defend yourself against it." Seth spent most of the evening speaking to us about our beliefs in an unsafe universe, and how we believe our world and our species to be unsafe and untrustworthy. "Now, the one-line official consciousness with which you are familiar says, 'The world is not safe. I cannot trust it. Nor can I trust the conditions of experience or the conditions of my own existence, nor can I trust myself.' "

As I listened, Seth's words rang true. I began to see an image of myself as Chicken Little, running through my childhood, shouting internally, "The sky is falling, the sky is falling," without saying it out loud. How crystal clear it all appeared to me now. I had never analyzed it before, but as a child I rarely if ever felt completely safe. That is why I worried so. The more I examined my life, the more apparent it became. If I had not felt unsafe, I would not have feared so much danger in all the events of my life, nor would I have experienced so much tension and anxiety in my body. Again, I had no idea of the origin of this fear. My parents, especially my mother, created such a protective loving environment that I could not blame them.

When I was a small child I believed in the magic of the universe. I believed in fairy tales and in the possibility of miracles. The world seemed to be full of color and song. As I grew into adolescence I was confronted with the world of facts, current events, and "real reality," which I was taught was the only clear and correct picture of reality. My dreams and fairy tales had nothing to do with the official world in which I had my existence. Although I had always resisted reading the newspaper or listening to the news on television, as a young woman I basically came to accept the picture of reality that the official world presented. From that time on it was as if something had died inside of me. The world became more black and white and ominous.

It was after my four years of illness that I began to question that black and white world again. I had to go beyond the official world of doctors and medicine in my desperate search for a cure and I had returned with a lot more than I had bargained for. Along with receiving enough healing energy to start the healing process in my liver, I also opened a door into the world of inner reality.

- 8 -

How the Utilization of These
Ideas Changed my Life

After many months of reading and studying the Seth teachings, I realized that I had to deal with my feelings of fear and inadequacy. I therefore began working with the Five-Phase Healing Program I had developed on a daily basis. After using meditation and breathing as a means of relaxing and opening my mind, I proceeded to focus on a suggestion and visualization. Each day I implanted the belief that my being was good and that my universe was safe. As a result I was able to begin the process of changing my beliefs—feeling less afraid of experience and more satisfied with myself.

Because the issues of worth and safety were so crucial for me, my life began to change subtly in response to the new suggestions. I gradually began to come out of my shell. Tentatively I began to talk about my operation.

On May 11, 1976, my father died unexpectedly of a heart attack. My mother, my siblings, and I experienced shock and grief as we came together to share our huge loss. Herman Perl had been so strong and vital that we could not imagine life without him. His death precipitated a lot of changes.

In November of that year Steve and I separated. It was he who finally said we could no longer go on in this unfulfilling relationship. Although I had secretly hoped for something like this, the prospect of losing Steve and my life on the farm, coming, as it did, so soon after losing my father, frightened me. Steve and I discussed the impossibility of continuing our marriage. We both knew that we had been lacking way too much joy and satisfaction. Although we truly cared for each other, our marriage was not nourishing enough for either of us.

Oddly, I felt terrified and grateful at the same time. I knew that Steve was giving me the second chance I had wanted. I realized that if I had made the move, I would have been responsible for destroying the business we ran on our farm. I would have felt terribly guilty about doing that to Steve. Now, with him making that move, I was free to embark on a new life, without guilt. As he drove me back to my mother's home I told him that I knew someday I would thank him, but that at that moment I felt disoriented and confused.

When I awoke the next day, I felt even more confused and lost. I was used to my life with Steve and I had no idea what I would do with myself now. I had lived in the country for four years, feeling closer to my animals than to most people. I was still close to my sister and brothers, who had all spent time with Steve and me at the farm. As far as friends went, however, I had few.

I knew, however, that the time had come to begin a new life for myself.

I decided to move to Manhattan. I knew Greenwich Village would be right for me, and so I went about the business of finding an apartment. It was only six months after my father's death and my mother was confused as she rode the subways with me to see some apartments. Six months ago we were both married women, and now here we were looking at tiny dives that my mother thought weren't fit for a rat. I felt excited, exhilarated, and scared.

I sublet a small, furnished apartment on Carmine Street and on December 1 moved in with my four small dogs—much to my mother's apprehension. I was ready to begin a new life, on my own. With the removal of my father's strong hand from my life, I felt truly on my own.

During this time I called Jane to inform her about the separation. She was very warm and supportive, supplying me with names and phone numbers of some of the regular class members who lived in New York City. She told me that she felt that one in particular would be very helpful to me.

I called Rich Kendall that night and within a very short time we became close friends. Rich was easy to talk to, enormously playful and funny. He seemed to know everyone who had attended the Seth classes and he introduced me to a lot of other people as well. I also dated occasionally. I began to think about meaningful ways to spend my time. I continued with my daily meditation and belief work, and all the while my life was changing around me.

I still found it frightening to tell people, especially men, about my ileostomy, but I was telling them nonetheless. I discovered that few people were as critical as I. Moreover, my beliefs about my body had changed more than I had realized. I still saw my ileostomy as a problem, but I made a separation in my mind between it and me. I knew now that my being amounted to more than any one part, and that although I was not particularly happy about this part, it didn't on the other hand diminish my value or beauty. I began to believe that I deserved to be loved by someone whose love I could easily return, and I did not feel that I would marry again unless I fell deeply in love.

I started to consider the idea of teaching Seth classes. I assumed that a lot of people were interested in Seth who had never had the opportunity to attend regular Seth classes during the time in which Jane held them.

I phoned Jane to ask her what she thought about the idea of my teaching. I was delighted to hear that she was all for it. I began to organize my ideas.

In January of 1977 I was using the Ouija board by myself, trying to get information for a troubled friend. The board kept spelling out the kind of motherly advice I would have given my friend. I felt rather foolish, as if I were making the entire communication up in my head. Then the planchette moved to the letter *G* and at the same time the name Jerry popped into my mind. "Does the name Jerry mean anything to you?" I asked Larry, who replied that it had no meaning for him at all. But I couldn't help thinking about that name. "Doesn't the name Jerry begin with a *J*?" I thought. "Why would the planchette pick out the letter *G* if the name I'm getting in my head is Jerry?" Throughout the next day this bothered me; somehow I couldn't get it out of my mind.

Later that day Rich came by to see me. He told me of a

friend of his, who, like the rest of us, was very much into the Seth material. He said that his friend had expressed a strong interest in meeting me. He went on to describe him in great detail, and then asked if he should give him my phone number. "Well, what's his name?" I asked, to which Rich replied, "Jerry."

"Give him the number," I said without hesitation.

Jerry contacted me a day later. We made a date to meet the following evening at my apartment and then go out to eat in the neighborhood. It turned out that Jerry lived just two blocks away.

I liked him immediately. He was tall, dark, and handsome, and exuded a sense of strength and trust. He was intelligent, and more important to me, he knew a lot about Seth and creating your own reality. When I told him I planned to teach a Seth class, he was supportive and enthusiastic. He offered to make me copies of all of his Seth tapes, which was a wonderful idea. I had only recorded a few sessions myself and hadn't yet figured out a format for my classes. It now occurred to me that the Seth tapes could be the finest teaching tool imaginable. We talked and figured out that he had stopped attending Seth classes regularly around the time that I began attending, which explained why I had met so many of his friends and not him. He was in his first year of law school, and was also in business with his father.

I hadn't consciously planned to become seriously involved with anyone so quickly after ending a seven-year marriage. But Jerry was so special. He had unique qualities that drew me to him. I found that the other men I met didn't affect me like Jerry did and I sensed that this relationship could possibly be an important one for me.

I decided to tell Jerry about the ileostomy right away. In the past I had always waited until the very last minute, but Jerry was different. On our first date we spent the evening talking and getting to know each other and I felt that we were, above all, open and honest with each other. We spoke about my illness. I didn't have the courage to talk about the surgery. I did tell Jerry that there was something I wanted to tell him, but did not feel comfortable to talk about yet. I remember feeling concerned that this knowledge might scare him away. By our second date, a few evenings later, I knew we were both looking at a potentially serious relationship, and if Jerry couldn't handle the ileostomy, I wanted to know now. I had grown enough to believe that any man who couldn't handle my situation wasn't man enough for me. Nonetheless I feared rejection.

By the time he arrived at my apartment I was pacing the floor. Lighting up one cigarette after another, I let Jerry into my small apartment and told him I had to talk about my problem. He sat down on the couch and listened intently as I fumbled around, trying to find pleasant words to describe what to me was a most unpleasant situation.

Jerry tried hard to keep his composure. I saw his eyes glance away from me momentarily as he began to get the picture, but for the most part he was difficult to read. We went out to dinner and basically had a nice evening, but we were both subdued. Jerry had been caught off guard and was now trying to sort through all that I had told him. I was afraid that I would lose him after all, and I felt naked and embarrassed. "Maybe I should have waited to tell him until he liked me more," I thought, but I knew this wasn't true. Relationships had to be handled openly and honestly from the start.

I didn't see or hear from Jerry for two weeks. I called and invited him once to dinner but he declined. He said he was going skiing for a couple of days and would call me when he returned. During this time I concluded that Jerry and I would probably just be friends. Although I hadn't completely given up on him, I felt he was backing away. I decided he was a nice guy to have as a friend, though, and I should definitely take him up on his offer to make Seth tapes for my class. With that in mind I called him the next Monday morning. To my surprise he said he was just about to call me and ask me out to dinner.

We had a nice time, but I still couldn't read him. He seemed to be interested in me, but he was holding back. I didn't know if this was because he cared about me and feared coming on too strong, or if he was scared of my body, or if he wasn't all that interested. Maybe he just wanted to pursue a friendship with me. But I knew I wanted more than friendship with him.

February 5, 1977, was my twenty-sixth birthday. I gave myself a party and invited all my new friends. Of course that included Jerry.

Needless to say, I was very jumpy. I knew Jerry and I would spend a night together soon, or not at all. Something had to give in this relationship. The vibrations between us were not what I would call platonic.

The party was scheduled for eight P.M. By nine practically everyone had arrived, except Jerry. My fear that he might not come at all mounted as ten o'clock approached. Finally at about ten-thirty he arrived with two friends who he said had kept him waiting. "Likely story," I thought, but I was enormously relieved anyway. The remainder of the party was filled with anticipation for both Jerry and me. When the last guest said good night we were finally alone. We both knew that the time had come for us to become lovers. Naturally we both felt ill at ease and I was reluctant to remove my clothing. My neighbor had lent me a sexy negligée that covered my appliance adequately, and this was how I dressed for bed that night, and for many years to come.

That night sealed the bond between us. We have been together ever since. I now had a satisfying relationship. My next intention was to begin filling my need for meaningful work.

I remember how fearful my mother was on the night that I opened my door to ten strangers who had answered my ad in the *Village Voice* about a Seth class. I had only spoken to these people on the phone, but felt certain that I would have no problems. The class went beautifully. I am still in contact with some of these people.

The classes became ongoing. Because of the enormous interest in Seth, I began to receive numerous phone calls from people who heard about the classes. I believe they were helpful and inspirational to many people, and certainly they helped me continue to build upon my positive beliefs. Listening week after week to Seth speak about the value of my being, my worth and right to joy, further reinforced my sense of power. I began to feel more confident. I made sure I meditated and worked with my beliefs daily.

As time went on, my self-awareness grew. I could now look into my mind every morning and see the beliefs that were seeding my emotions. Every time emotions seemed to come upon me that I didn't understand, I could discover their source within my beliefs. I also came to see the same two key issues underlying most of the others that arose: either I felt I wasn't good enough, that my energy was not to be trusted, or that I wasn't safe enough, and the universe was not to be trusted. As I continued to work with the ideas that my being was good as well as safe, I found that I was becoming a more happy and secure person.

In the spring of 1977, I moved into Jerry's apartment and that fall we moved to a larger, more comfortable space. There I taught Seth classes twice a week and held many private sessions. I felt now, for the first time in my life, that I was where I wanted to be, doing what I wanted to do. Jerry and I were beginning to understand each other, and I felt content and complete in our life together. I had love, meaningful work, a wonderful family, and a terrific group of friends. Jerry and I were married on September 15, 1979, in Las Vegas, shortly after my divorce became final. The only incomplete part of the picture was the ileostomy. Although I could accept it more, it was still a source of sadness for me. Yet I honestly couldn't imagine undergoing surgery again. All I remembered of surgery was enormous pain and sickness. I was certain that I would always be denied surgery to reconnect my bowel.

On the night of September 29, 1979, Jane Roberts held a small Seth class in her home. It was the last class that any of us attended, the last tape and transcript that we acquired. As always we were all enthralled by the power of Seth's wisdom and love as he spoke to us about trusting our everyday impulses. He spoke to Jerry, whom he had always referred to as "the Indian," instructing him to trust his impulses in our marriage.

As the evening drew to a close we mingled and talked. At this time Sue Watkins walked over to Jerry and told him that he still reminded her of Kurt Vonnegut. My ears perked up in excitement as I realized what was taking place. I hadn't even thought about the Kurt Vonnegut business since the day Jerry and I had met. And here I was married to him! How amazing, I thought, that I had felt so much for him on our first meeting in Jane's kitchen. How incredible the way our inner self knows and feels things before our conscious mind. My number-one dream had come true. I wondered whether any of this could have happened if I hadn't changed my beliefs. In my heart I knew that it couldn't have, and that all of this was the reward.

In January of 1982 Jerry and I adopted our first son. Because I had never used birth control and had never missed a period, I assumed I was not overly fertile. I felt that my body, which was maintained by a lot less intestine than the average person's, had its own wisdom and would have conceived if it wanted to. I therefore had no desire to pursue any medical treatment to bring about conception, and began to ask the universe to deliver my children to me through another means.

I meet many people who make painful choices to avoid adopting a child because they believe a relationship with an adopted child is somehow less sacred than a biological one. I feel sorry for them. The bond that I share with my boys is stronger than blood. It is another example of how our beliefs determine the conditions of our lives, what happens to us, and what does not.

Fortunately, as a result of our beliefs, Jerry and I now have a thriving family. Our two boys have already given us enormous joy and satisfaction. Being a mother has added a deeply nourishing dimension to my life. Each day I live I am more grateful for the lives of my sons, and for their presence in mine.

- 9 -

Reconnective Surgery

When my first son was about fourteen months old, I began to go through a difficult time. From the day he was given to me I had insisted on taking care of him completely and had never left him with a baby-sitter. I believed that I was a better mother if I never left him. It was easy enough to do when he was a tiny baby because he slept a lot, and when he was up, I was fascinated by him. Now, as he was becoming more active and demanding, I began to feel swamped and angry. I would go through the entire day trying not to lose my patience. When at the end of the day I finally did, I would feel terrible for the rest of the night. I started to fall into a pattern of wanting to be the perfect mother, which to me meant never being frustrated or curt with my child, and then feeling miserable because I couldn't attain it. I began to feel either frustrated or guilty all of the time.

The easiest solution would have been to get some part-time help with Aaron so I could have some time to myself. However, I wasn't ready to admit this, so instead I got hives. I started breaking out with enormous swellings that forced my eyes shut and my body to itch all over.

The only explanation I could think of was that my rectum was still intact from the last surgery. My doctors had warned me that a rectum disconnected from the bowel was danger-ous. Dr. Marvin had always been in favor of removal, and because I had quite frequently suffered pain in my lower back and abdomen (as a result of swelling or blockages in the disconnected colon and rectum that remained), I sometimes considered it. But the idea of facing surgery only to make the ileostomy permanent didn't sit well with me. Now, however, I was frightened. I had always argued that no part of my body was going to become ill, connected or not, as my blood still flowed into it and my blood was too full of healthy suggestions to fail me now. But I wondered. Could these hives be the result of something really terrible happening in my body? And if such was the case, what did that say about my beliefs and all that I thought I had accomplished? Could I, in fact, be unhealthy?

As a result of the hives and my fear, I allowed myself to be examined for bowel disease for the first time in many years. All of my favorite tests were run. The results showed that my bowels were one hundred percent healthy and not related to the hives. My fears rose again, however, when a few days later Dr. Marvin informed me that he wasn't pleased with the result of one of my blood tests. He said that it seemed to indicate liver illness, and that further blood tests as well as a sonogram were necessary. My first reaction was anger. I vehemently told him that I would not be further tested and that I knew that I was well. However, soon my anger gave way to fear as the doctor said that I shouldn't try to hide from the truth. "Think it over," he said, "and call me back." I hung up and found myself overwhelmed with different reactions.

I was experiencing plenty of energy and exuberance. How could I feel so much energy if my liver was in serious trouble? Isn't liver disease always accompanied by weakness? And furthermore, when I submitted to blood tests ten years back, hadn't Dr. Marvin then found the same liver abnormality? At the time my family and I had undergone a week-long scare, waiting for results from a second, more extensive set of blood tests.

I was living on my farm in Chemung then, experiencing the same doubts and fears as now. I paced back and forth in the kitchen, waiting for that inevitable phone call that would tell me if I was well.

Two nights before I received the test results in Chemung, I had a dream. Jane Roberts appeared to me and said, "If you believed in the validity of your own experience, then you would know that you are well. You would trust what

you know and you would have no fear of the blood test!"
The results showed that the liver was indeed well, and there
was no real explanation as to why the first, more general
liver test appeared abnormal.

I now thought that this could easily be the same abnormality that Dr. Marvin uncovered before. "Surely, I couldn't
be ill. It couldn't be possible," I reasoned as I paced, back
and forth, my small son at my feet. "And liver disease, of
all things. Does this mean that my life might end soon?" I
picked up my son. I wondered how this could be happening
to me. Surely I wanted to be here, clearly I had all the
elements in my life that I needed, and I was still meditating
and working on my beliefs every day. I wondered what
could be behind this. I was stumped. I was also extremely
upset. I cried for a while, feeling unbearably sorry for myself. Then an amazing thought occurred to me. "If I'm
well," I thought, "then I have nothing to worry about, but if
I truly am sick, and might die sooner than I had planned, I'd
better not waste any more time being miserable!" That evening Jerry and I went out with a group of our friends. I
found the entire evening somehow more alive and wonderful in light of its evanescence.

Further tests again proved that my liver was fine. The
hives cleared up a few weeks later. I decided to get some
part-time help with my son, which allowed me to engage in
some of my own projects. It was now the spring of 1983. I
decided that in the fall I would look into my bowel situation, as I had already gone through so many of the dreaded
tests as a result of my hives.

Right after Thanksgiving my mother and I went to see
Doctors Baum and Marvin. It was wonderful to see David
again after all these years. Although more than a decade
had passed, he didn't look a day older. I was confident that
he would give me his best advice. I had already chosen not
to use him as my surgeon, not because I didn't trust him,
but because I wanted to eliminate all past associations surrounding surgery.

I told David of my desire to deal with this situation once
and for all. I asked him if he thought reconnection was
possible, and if it was advisable. He said that it might work,
but I would have to bear in mind that if it didn't the

ileostomy would have to be made permanent by removal of my rectum. The idea of going through surgery twice, only to end up where I had been, seemed like an unbearable punishment to me . . . and yet how could I not take the chance?

My mother then asked David if he knew exactly how much colon I had left. We both remembered Barry saying, just after the surgery, that not enough tissue remained to make the temporary opening and that David had done something unusual. David said that there was enough tissue to warrant reconnection. Dr. Marvin disagreed. He felt that the amount of diarrhea I would have to live with after the reconnection was done could make me a slave to the bathroom. He also mentioned the greater risk of recurrence with reconnection. That did not concern me. What did concern me was the idea of living in the bathroom.

However, we had been merely seeking advice and we weren't planning to use either David or Dr. Marvin. I wanted to hear from the people who might actually do the work. Dan Present and Irwin Gelernt had both been strongly recommended to us. The first was known to be one of the best gastroenterologists in Manhattan, and the second was reputed to be a brilliant surgeon.

I phoned Dr. Present's office the next day, but he wasn't available. That night at nine our phone rang, and an easy pleasant voice introduced himself as Dan Present. I poured out my entire story (including my experience with Harry Edwards and healing). Dan listened, said he couldn't comment on my healing story but that reconnection was certainly possible. When confronted with my fears concerning diarrhea, he explained that there were medications to regulate such conditions. He allayed my fears about the amount of colon I had remaining. His confidence was infectious. He approved highly of Dr. Gelernt and said he'd be happy to work with him, and often did.

When Dr. Present saw my X rays, he said that I certainly had enough ileum left for reconnection. After a general examination, he said I appeared to be in very good health. The next step would be for me to see Dr. Gelernt, while Dr. Present would review the results of my blood tests. When we left the doctor's office I began again to wrestle with my fears. I did not know it, but I was about to face the last struggle with my resistance to surgery.

"This is craziness," I thought, "my life is going fine. If I take a chance with this surgery, I could make a mess of things. I've already gone through the toughest years with an ileostomy, made all the adjustments when they were most difficult to make. Why should I bother to try and change it now?" There were a zillion reasons for me to forget the whole idea, but I knew that I could not. One way or another the internal structure of my bowels had to be altered. Either I could attempt to reconnect my rectum to my ileum, or opt to remove my rectum completely.

Feeling very upset and frightened that evening, I informed Jerry and my mother that I was going to forget about the entire situation. I was certain that I could not deal with the surgery. I would put the matter off for a few years and worry about it then. In my own mind I knew that I was growling and blowing off steam, but it felt comforting to assume that I had the choice to call the whole thing off anytime I wanted to.

When I awoke in the morning I felt quite different. If I was going to deal with this situation, and I was, then I certainly wanted to try to reconnect my rectum. Somehow in the light of day all of this seemed attainable. For the first time in years I indulged in fantasies of what it would feel like to possess my old body again. Before I knew what was happening, I had my heart set on reconnection. My new concern was that the doctors would discover some reason to discourage me.

I liked Dr. Gelernt. He exuded knowledge and confidence. I passed his inspection, and he saw no reason preventing me from undergoing reconnective surgery. He looked in his calendar, said that he could make time and scheduled me for two weeks after the new year. Then we returned to Dr. Present's office. Dan confirmed that my blood tests checked out normally and agreed that we should go ahead with the surgery. He even said that if he had seen me in the past, he would have encouraged me to take this action sooner.

Nothing stood in my way now. We were in the middle of December, and I had only one month to wait. During this time I went through a lot of ups and downs but, having made up my mind to face surgery, I didn't falter again. All of a sudden my ileostomy annoyed me more.

During this time Doctors Gelernt and Present tried to obtain my past medical records. Oddly, none seemed to exist. Dr. Gelernt assumed that because I had a temporary ileostomy, I must have at least one foot of colon attached to my rectum.

I checked into Mt. Sinai Hospital in Manhattan on January 10, 1984. I remember it as if it was yesterday. With my arm wrapped tightly around Jerry's we walked slowly down the long hospital corridor as an orderly took us up to my room, complete with a view of the park. "I may be reduced to helplessness for a while," I thought, "but I'm going to walk out of here on my own two feet." As a result of working with my beliefs, I had found the courage to face what at one time seemed impossible to me. I was scared, but not too scared to make this change in my life.

As I walked slowly up to my room, savoring those last few moments before I became a patient, I could barely believe what I was doing. I didn't know where the courage came to go through with this, but it was there.

In retrospect, I can see that my ability to face this reality was fostered by my working with beliefs, particularly in the area of safety. Years of addressing the issue of fear had lightened fear's hold upon me. By suggesting to myself that I was safe and protected, I slowly whittled away at my fear until I was free to take this action.

As I sat in my hospital bed, waiting for the stretcher that would take me down the long corridor to the surgical rooms, I was amazed at my composure and confidence. My family surrounded me, as my siblings and I chanted together. I felt reassured that my healer friend in Britain, Ray Branch, had been informed of the surgery. Ray had worked with Harry Edwards for many years prior to Harry's death in 1976. I knew that Ray would direct all the help possible to me now. I was also receiving healing energy from Eva and Eugene Graf. Friends of my brother Richard's, they are the founders of the Center of the Light, in Great Barrington, Massachusetts. This is a center where many healers live, teach, and work together. I was fortunate to have many of them focus their attention on me. My family, friends, and students sent their love, and when the stretcher finally did come to collect me, my attitude was one of faith and trust. "Put me out and do your thing to me," I thought, "I will trust that I will be safe."

My mother and Jerry walked alongside my stretcher for as long as they were allowed, and then we kissed good-bye, just in front of the restricted area.

As usual I waited on my stretcher for something to happen, wishing that the sedative had made me less aware. A few minutes later I was wheeled into an operating room. I remember Dr. Gelernt walking in and the huge surge of confidence I felt. "Please put me together again," I thought.

I had made Jerry promise that he would come into the recovery room as soon as he was allowed. I wanted to know if the surgery had been successful. I had an eerie feeling that the situation inside my body might not be just as it should. I didn't fear illness, but I did worry about the amount of tissue remaining. I remembered what Barry had said back in 1969 about the temporary hook-up. I couldn't help wondering if Dr. Gelernt was going to find what he expected. I kept saying that I feared he would discover a can of worms inside and hoped that things were going to work out.

When Dr. Gelernt opened me up, he did not find the foot of colon he expected to find. Instead he found four inches of colon connected to twenty-one inches of ileum, an unusual hook-up indeed. Apparently in my last surgery David found himself with too little colon to make a temporary hook-up. He didn't have the heart to remove my rectum either, which would have rendered the ileostomy irreversible. He therefore connected ileum to colon in order to make the piece of remaining disconnected tissue longer. In this way he was able to create what is called a temporary hook-up. Although difficult to explain, I will try.

When this type of surgery is done, the tissues that are disconnected from the rest of the bowel (the rectum, colon, and sometimes ileum) are not just left lying around inside the body. Instead the loose end is tied off at the abdomen. An opening is made on the abdomen so that fluids and air can be released. If there is not sufficient tissue remaining to make this opening, then the rectum is often removed, and the ostomy is permanent.

David figured out a way to avoid a permanent ileostomy by substituting ileum for colon. Nonetheless, when Dr. Gelernt discovered this, he could have decided against reconnection. The colon is the large bowel and the ileum is the small bowel. They work differently. The colon works as a reservoir. It holds water. How much water could a four-inch colon hold? Dr. Gelernt took all of this into consideration and chose to reconnect my bowel.

When I became aware in the recovery room, I somehow knew that my bowel had been reconnected. How I knew this, I still don't understand. Soon Jerry was allowed to see me and he confirmed my feeling and told me everything looked fine. I was greatly relieved that the pain from the surgery was certainly bearable. It had nothing in common with my former surgeries.

The next two weeks were not easy ones—except compared to what I had feared them to be. My brother Richard, who lived near the hospital, visited early every morning to check my progress or massage my feet. I came to rely on his encouragement and visits throughout the long days of recovery. Naturally I felt quite ill. My bowels did not work for about ten days, and when they did I could barely find my way out of the bathroom. Fortunately, within a few days, my doctors started giving me medication to slow down bowel function. It made all the difference in the world. What could have been an unbearable living situation changed radically. For the first time in many years I came to see that medicine can be a marvelous thing.

You can imagine the feelings of deep satisfaction and liberation I felt as a result of this final surgery after fifteen years of living with an ileostomy.

It appears now that I will probably take medication for the rest of my life. Normal colons are ten feet long; mine is only four inches. Considering this, I feel grateful for the medication that makes my colon behave as if it were normal. Perhaps someday my colon will function better, thus eliminating the need for medication, but I am not concerned about it. The medication is a very small price to pay for liberation from my ileostomy.

On the other hand, I want to make it clear that I do not see living with an ileostomy as the worst thing in the world. To be perfectly honest, since the event of reconnective surgery, my life has changed very little. I'm married to the same man, I'm busy with the raising of my two children. I've maintained most of the same friends and interests. Of course I experience a physical and psychological freedom that I do appreciate. If I had been stronger, however, I might have been able to achieve it anyway. The fact is, the most important aspects of my life have not changed.

When I look back on my ileostomy, I can see how in many ways, it was positive. Certainly it, and my entire bout with illness, made me question what really matters in life, and what does not. I came to see that how you view what happens to you is much more important than what actually happens. If you truly love and trust yourself, you can learn how to make the most out of life, even if life doesn't always go as you had intended it.

Adversity can go a long way toward developing values and priorities. Life-threatening situations make you focus on what matters most to you. The petty annoyances of life are no longer worth bothering about. The key here is to realize and focus upon what brings joy and satisfaction to you. Adversity need not be a prerequisite to straightening out your beliefs and attitudes. Examining and changing limiting beliefs, however, is a prerequisite to good health and a satisfying life experience. As you can see from observing my life, as I began to change my beliefs, the scope of my experience altered radically. I stopped feeling like a victim and started feeling like a creator. I am not saying that things never go wrong in my life, or that I never experience unhappiness. I am saying, however, that my overall experience is joyful and challenging. When I do experience difficulties, at least I now have some tools to rely upon.

The same will hold true for you. As you work with altering your beliefs, you will discover that you become more powerful and in control of your life. You will be able to make changes you thought were impossible. I hope that through observing my life, you will feel encouraged about the possibilities for change that exist within your own!

Part III

- 10 -

My Work with Others

Over the years I have worked with many people. While my ideas were developing, there was always a constant flow of interaction between myself and others. Naturally, through experience my program became more specific and finely tuned. However, the most significant message that I can extrapolate from reviewing the case histories before me, is that people got better who were willing to make use of the tools at their disposal: people who, for whatever reasons and situations, decided to take the responsibility for changing their lives.

The particular method was not the most important factor. The intent, desire, and effort applied was. My intent was always to help others. Although when I first began teaching, I had not formulated my ideas, those students who were ready to create change in their lives, did. Some of them made contact with Ray Branch in England. (Ray worked for many years with Harry Edwards. At the time of Harry Edwards's death in 1976 Ray took over the Harry Edwards Spiritual Healing Sanctuary.) Others became deeply involved in Seth and quite literally changed their entire outlook. Some students became devoted to the practice of daily meditation. Practically everyone became involved with visualization, employing the use of "energy exercise" cassettes that I made for my classes. As I added something new to my own practice, I added it to my teachings.

It is willingness and desire that create change. Any of the different methods outlined in this book can be used to bring about change. Any of the wonderful healers, psychic, holistic or medical, can be called upon for help. Just don't forget that *you* are the catalyst. You have to accept responsibility for your present situation and make the internal decision to change. Then you can go about using people, places, and methods to help you bring that change about.

In the following pages you will read about real people who I have worked with. You will be able to see which aspects of the program they used and how their lives changed as a result. You will also see the many different ways that I have approached these cases. One factor, however, holds true for all of them. My desire to help others comes from the heart. I genuinely care for the people who come to me and together we seek to understand the cause within their difficulties. I constantly strive to open people's minds and hearts to the fact that there is more to life than what meets the eye.

It is my belief that benign universal energy exists. Seth refers to this energy as "All-that-is." Naturally, upbringing or culture determine how you see or refer to this energy. I do not feel that one way of believing is better or closer to truth than another. However, I think it is important to understand that if this energy exists, it exists for all of us. Each of us can send out a plea to the universe. If we are willing to make the changes that are required of us, we eliminate blocks to the magical healing power of the universe. After all that I have seen, I never limit possibility. With that in mind, let's take a look at a few actual case histories!

Joyce Liechenstein is fifty-two years old. She attended my first Seth class in 1977. At the time she was experiencing depression and chronic upper respiratory infections. "On an emotional level, I was suffering from low self-esteem," Joyce recalls. "I just didn't feel good enough about myself. Physically, I was getting ill quite often. It seemed as though I had the flu at least two or three times a year. I ran high fevers and was taking medication to help me feel better." In my classes, along with teaching the Seth concept that you create your own reality, we talked about the power of beliefs and the power of suggestion. We discussed ways in which our concentration and suggestions formed our health as well as our physical experience.

"Through the Seth teachings I realized that I had to work with my beliefs. When I began affirming that I was worthy of health, my emotional health and physical health improved substantially. This is how I began to make these changes. Every morning as I left for work I used the front door of my apartment building as a trigger to remind me to mentally repeat a positive suggestion to myself. I would do this each day, without exception, as I went from my home to the bus stop. I would say, over and over, 'I am worthy of health.' In the afternoon I would take approximately five minutes to mentally repeat to myself, 'My point of power is in the present.' I remember that it was about one year later when I became aware of the fact that I hadn't been sick for a while. It was as if I just woke up to realize that I felt better about myself and my life."

Joyce began working as a therapist in 1976. After becoming a regular member of my Seth group in 1977, Joyce began to implement the Seth teachings in her work: "The Seth teachings became the backbone of my work. As a therapist I now realize that the point of all psychotherapy is to first understand the cause behind negative feelings. Depression, for example, can happen when someone is constantly suggesting negative things to herself. It could be that a person has suffered a negative experience in childhood. This experience may be forgotten but because of it the person may have drawn a conclusion about herself. Whenever possible it is best to uncover the experience. In any event, it is necessary to look at the conclusion that has been drawn, to question it and to change it to a more positive conclusion. Through reevaluation and suggestions you try to change negative conclusions and attitudes. This is representative of the way my own therapists have worked with me and how I work with myself and my clients.

"I still work with affirmations on a daily basis. I begin my day by stating an affirmation that is a combination of affirmations I have either read or that have been given to me. This is what I suggest: 'I am filling myself with pure white light so that only love and purposefulness, wisdom and health, healing energy, peace, and joy will be here now. I release all my past, fears, doubts, negatives, relationships, and inner self to the light. I am a light being. My true nature is light. I radiate light from my light center throughout my being to everyone and everything. I now step into a crystal cathedral of light where my angel guides are and the hierarchy is. They send me love and energy and I am well and strong. Perfect thyroid function, perfect circulation, all the energy I need. All past imprints of trauma in my cells are released and my cells are returning to a state of perfect joy and harmony. Only love and light can come here now and only love and light can stay. I receive this, so be it and so it is. Thank you God for everything.'

"This is the affirmation that I am fond of using. People can make up their own, of course. I do find that affirmation following meditation is even more powerful as meditation induces an altered state in which the mind is more open to suggestion. As I think about it, working with meditation, affirmation, and prayer has been the greatest factor in creating change in my life."

Joyce now enjoys excellent health, both mentally and physically. She is a counselor, psychotherapist, certified NLP practitioner of hypnosis, certified Reiki therapist, certified MariEl healer, and an interfaith minister. She works with individuals, couples and groups, training them in meditation, creative visualization, hypnosis, and self-healing.

Joyce and I have remained in touch over the years. I know of all the wonderful changes she has instituted in her life. She is a dedicated and sincere teacher and healer. I highly recommend her work. (For further information about Joyce, see references.)

Susan Caryl is forty-one years old. She is a full-time single parent and an ex-professional dancer/roller skater. Susan and I met through our children. Around the time her daughter was twelve months old, Susan began to experience pain in her chest. Finding the idea of something being seriously wrong frightening, Susan attempted to ignore the pain. Six months later the pain was too acute to ignore and Susan was forced to see a doctor. An X ray revealed a mass on Susan's lung. The doctors saw no other choice but to operate on Susan in order to perform a biopsy. The idea of surgery absolutely terrified Susan. She was very disturbed and told the doctor that she wanted to postpone the biopsy for at least one week, during which time she contacted me as well as other teachers and healers.

The following week Susan decided to pay a visit to her mother's internist. While examining Susan, he noticed a node protruding on Susan's neck. Susan was sure that it hadn't been visible the day before. Fortunately, the biopsy could be taken from this protruding node, thus eliminating a major surgical procedure.

The biopsy indicated that Susan definitely had Hodgkin's disease. Her doctors informed her that her illness was treatable through chemotherapy and radiology.

In Susan's words, "The terror and shock of hearing that I was seriously ill was beyond my worst imaginings. I thought that I would collapse on the spot, but I had to think of my little girl. I knew how desperately she needed me to live and that I would do anything to become well."

Susan worked with physicians and cooperated with all medical treatment. I also contacted British healer Ray Branch on her behalf. Susan and I began working together to create visualizations of health in her body. We envisioned pure white light shining through Susan's body and clearing her of all illness. We worked with suggestion and affirmations. Because Susan is particularly fond of crystals, we worked with crystal meditations. We envisioned healing energy emanating from a crystal that Susan held in her hand and entering her body. I made a point of seeing that Susan had a crystal to wear around her neck as well. In Susan's words, "I never went to a treatment without holding a healing crystal in my hand. The cold feeling that I experienced when the poisonous chemicals entered my body shook me to the very core of my being. I held on to the crystal as if it were my dearest friend."

During the early stages of Susan's illness we talked a lot. Susan knew all about my history, which helped her believe that healing energy could indeed be directed to her—energy capable of helping her overcome her illness. We also discussed the necessity of a strong mental position regarding her treatment. "I realized that if I was going to take this treatment, I would have to work along with the treatment rather than against it. Whenever I went for a treatment or took medication, I said to myself, 'Everything that I take or swallow turns into health and beauty.' I also repeated another suggestion to myself, which went something like this: 'Anything that does not belong in my body will perish—any foreign parts that do not keep my body well and whole will disintegrate.' "

Susan underwent treatment consistently for ten months. During those long months she had some terrifying moments—days when she was very ill from the treatments and other times when she feared for the well-being of her small child. Susan says, "When this would happen I would do what Sheri calls 'going back to basics.' I would take a warm bath and try to relax with deep breathing. I would look at my thoughts and notice that I had been thinking very negatively about my illness. I would then make an effort to think positively. I would picture my life ahead of me and myself well and happy. I would see my body cleared of all illness. These thoughts became my nourishment. Sometimes I would call Sheri just for her encouragement. I knew that she would help me to see all the positive possibilities. I feel that it is a combination of many things that helped me to become well. My attitude and my positive suggestions helped me respond to and handle the treatments. I had recently lost a close friend to illness, so I knew that everyone does not make it. Sheri tried to help me focus on the positive aspects of my life that did exist—my daughter being the most important one. I know now that my strongest motivation to keep alive was my daughter. I was not willing to give that gift up. I truly believed that my daughter was given to me because we were intended to live a full and happy life together. Through working with Sheri's teachings relating to positive thinking, visualization, and affirmation, I was able to feel more in control in a very out-of-control situation. I had something of substance to believe in—myself, and the power of my own positive thoughts.

"After six months my tests showed real improvement. I was so relieved! I continued to use all my mental powers to see that things stayed that way. I took over my own correspondence with Ray Branch and continued to receive help from other teachers and healers who are friends of mine. You could say that I had many friends in high places praying for me. There is no question in my mind that the healing energy that was directed to me and my own effort to focus positively played a huge role in the happy outcome of my complete recovery!"

Since Susan's recovery she has remained healthy in all ways. Her lovely daughter is growing up beautifully, which is a credit to Susan as well. When I spoke with Susan just the other day, she told me, "Recently I went to see Arianne in a school play. As she sat there on the edge of the stage singing, 'That's What Friends Are For,' I was moved to tears. I realized how fortunate I am to be well and to have her in my life. Sometimes when life becomes bogged down with responsibility it is easy to forget your blessings. That day I was reminded of my own."

Susan says that she still works on a daily basis with positive thinking, visualizations, and affirmations, knowing that in this way she will ensure her continued spiritual and physical health.

Clarence Dougherty is thirty-five years old. He moved to the United States from Ecuador in 1968. When he first attended my earliest Seth class, he was not the confident secure individual that he is today. His beliefs about himself and his power were not as positive as they could be. In class he was given the opportunity to examine them. We discussed the nature of beliefs and how they form every aspect of our experience. We looked at ways to become aware of our personal belief structures and how to change beliefs that were producing undesirable results. "At the end of every class I would be filled with new ideas as to how to work on changing my beliefs. The classes were like a springboard on which I would jump into different directions. I was able to look within myself, and not be too afraid. It became the safety net that I needed to feel safe while looking at my fears. As a result I am more certain of my basic goodness, of my Godness."

We talked a lot in those classes about belief systems. Clarence, who had grown up with some very strict religious beliefs, began for the first time to examine them. "I think the biggest release has been the letting go of the overwhelming effect religion had upon me. It had been my belief that I had been born a sinner. Due to that belief I suffered from a lot of guilt. I felt that there was something wrong with my being, which caused me a lot of pain. As I began to examine that belief, I realized how foolish guilt was. I stopped blaming myself for my father's death. I was able to see the underlying purpose of every event in my life. I then understood how my father's death had contributed to my growth. I also came to see the roles my father and I played and how we touched each other's lives."

My classes also focused on visualization. We worked on visualizing health in our bodies and new beliefs taking form. Clarence used visualization to heal himself of intestinal tumors. "I had gone to my doctor because I was having abdominal pain. He had discovered two tumors on my intestines. My doctor tried treating them with medications but the treatment was not working. The tumors were growing. My doctor recommended an operation to remove them. We agreed that the operation would take place the following month. I was very frightened, because when you are told that you have to face surgery there seems to be no way out. My doctor seemed quite certain that this was the only solution. I felt backed against a wall. A few days later I realized that maybe I had a choice if I started working with my mental power. We had talked much in the Seth classes about the power each individual has to create health through their positive beliefs, I decided that if I had to have the surgery, I would, but in the meantime I began a daily visualization to try to heal myself. First, I used images from the Drano liquid cleaner commercial. Every day I imagined my intestines as clean as the pipes appeared in the commercial, after the liquid cleaner had been applied. Next, I used an idea from the movie *Fantastic Voyage*. In my mind I reduced myself to microscopic size and began a smooth journey through my intestines. Next, from a Certs commercial I borrowed the idea of skiing down smooth slopes of white pure snow. These slopes represented my intestines. I expected a happy journey to take place. I started my journey and from time to time would stop to talk to different 'people' who were welcoming me. These 'people' were my cells, to whom I would engage in what I call 'loving' talk. Often I would declare their power and beauty. At first I felt silly and foolish. My critical mind would think that I was just playing childrens' games. Although I believed that thoughts and images were powerful, I didn't really know just how powerful they were. There were days when my fear and doubts overwhelmed me and I seriously doubted that I would be able to help myself. Because I knew that I had nothing to lose I persevered. The more I did this visualization, the more convinced I became of the 'reality' of it. A month later I went back to see my doctor. I was not experiencing any more pain. Further tests were run, which showed that the tumors disappeared and the operation was no longer necessary. I was overjoyed. As a result of this experience I have really developed even greater respect for the power of my thoughts and visual images."

As time passed Clarence emerged as a happier and more self-satisfied person. He has assisted me many times in running my healing workshop. His lovely nature makes him a pleasure to know. His use of these ideas has always been inspirational to me. "The belief in the power I have to change my reality is more real to me now. As I gain awareness and consciously apply new beliefs, I bring about changes within myself. These changes, in turn, paint my world as more fun and beautiful to me. The more that I see my participation in the creation of my experiences, the safer I feel. I also have developed a greater love for myself."

Clarence's case history shows how working with beliefs, suggestion, and visualization can overcome both emotional and physical problems. As Clarence began to sort out some of his religious beliefs, he was emotionally freed. As he worked with visual images, he was able to heal his body. In my experience I have seen positive results take place in all types of situations. From insecurity to depression to severe physical conditions, I am always happy to hear of the miraculous changes my students report.

One of my first Seth-class students is a mime artist. One night in class she told a fascinating story. She explained to the class how every member in her family wore glasses and that approximately six months before discovering the Seth ideas she was beginning to have vision problems. She was very disturbed, but she had almost expected the problem. She finally went to purchase a pair of glasses, at which point she discovered the Seth books and began reading them. She instantly started working with suggestion and visualization. "I suggested that there was nothing wrong with my eyes and that my vision was strong. I visualized seeing objects very clearly." Within two months her vision cleared up dramatically and she threw the glasses away! A decade has passed since this healing took place. Lois still reports excellent vision!

SuZen, an artist-photographer, refers to herself as ageless. She began suffering from chronic ulcerative colitis in 1968. At the time, in SuZen's words, "I felt like a victim with no power or control over what was happening to my body." When her condition was diagnosed, SuZen was put on a form of sulfa medication, which she took for many years. Her diet was radically altered to very bland soft foods. She was hospitalized twice, and when her illness was at its worst, she was placed on cortisone, in addition to her already prescribed medicine. When her condition improved, she was able to eliminate the cortisone but continued to take the original medication.

In 1979 SuZen had another difficult bout with her colitis. At the same time she had seen posters for my class and had the impulse to call me. SuZen and I met and discussed her illness. SuZen was interested in finding another way to control her symptoms, fearing the harsh side effects of cortisone. I could certainly relate to how SuZen felt and shared my experience with her. She started attending my Seth classes as a step toward learning more about creating her own reality.

In the classes we talk at length about how you create your own experience through your beliefs, thoughts, and emotions. SuZen began to feel that maybe she could gain some control over her symptoms and decided not to rush off to her doctor for a cortisone prescription. At the end of every class I would lead the group in an energy exercise in which we envisioned white light entering us and healing us. We worked with the image of a pyramid, emanating healing energy that we could each absorb into ourselves. SuZen says, "I always found the energy exercises involving the use of white light and healing pyramids very calming. They helped me to relax and absorb healing energy."

SuZen's symptoms began to ease. Then she made a weekend trip to Boston. In her words, "I returned from Boston feeling well. As I entered my apartment building I saw a notice on the wall announcing that our rents were being raised twenty-seven percent. I immediately felt a pain in the pit of my gut. It was really at that point that I was able to make the connection between my thoughts and my physical body, especially in the area of money and survival. This awareness put me in touch with my need to focus my energy in the areas of abundance and safety. I realized that fear was undermining my peace of mind, which was affecting my health. As I began to look at these issues and work with affirmations, I found that my physical symptoms began to clear up. I would watch my mind. If I found that I was thinking negative thoughts, I would pluck those thoughts out and replace them with positive ones. Sometimes I would walk around town repeating positive suggestions to myself.

"Within a few months' time I was symptom free without going on the cortisone. Sometime after that I stopped all medication and was completely well for many years. During that time I experienced no pain and ate whatever foods I wanted. Then approximately a year and a half ago I had a small relapse. I was overworked and under an enormous amount of pressure. I didn't have the time to work with my spiritual self and I was feeling frustrated and angry. To make matters worse I felt unable to express my anger or frustration and held it tightly inside myself.

"It didn't take long before it backed up inside of me and began to produce symptoms. The difference was that at this point in my life I no longer felt like a victim. I knew that I had power to make changes and that I would not end up in the hospital again. I realized that if I did not take the time to work with fear and frustration, I became vulnerable again to illness. I began to work on relaxing, breathing, and meditating. I observed my thoughts and began to replace negative ones with positive ones. I began doing affirmations and visualizations as well. Two to three months later I began to feel wonderful again and have felt terrific since.

"What I learned from my short relapse, and I think it is very important, is that working with and changing your beliefs is an ongoing process. You may at times have to stop yourself to insert certain thoughts into your mind. Sometimes we forget the power of our thoughts. What is important for me now is that I know I am no longer a victim. I have the control, and when my illness returned briefly, I knew how to handle the situation. I think it is important for people to realize that there is much that they can do to control the state of their health and that they are not helpless."

SuZen says that she takes no medication today, eats whatever foods she desires, and feels wonderful. She is an excellent example of how healing from the inside out can work.

Julia Farley Davis is over seventy years old. She is a retired advertising executive, a widow, and a writer. She took my healing workshop in 1982 and again in 1983. Prior to attending my class, Julia had lost her husband. "The stress and trauma of losing a man I adored after twenty-five years of devotion was affecting my health and I was suffering from arthritis. I was withdrawn and confused about the future, frightened consciously for the first time in my life. My ties with God through my lifelong religion had broken when my beloved husband died." Although Julia mentioned that she was having trouble with arthritis, I was not aware of the depth of her pain. She was bright, beautiful, and cheerful, and I was therefore not in touch with her suffering.

In my workshop we discussed a person's own responsibility in creating satisfaction through working with inner resources. I taught the meditation technique that is introduced in Part III of this book. Time was then allotted to practice meditation and I directed the group in guided visualizations. For Julia, these ideas and techniques had a powerful effect. "Sheri's gentle leadership and spiritual understanding set me on a deep and committed new spiritual path, more individual and full of a satisfying serenity and peace. I learned to look inward, accepting total responsibility for each day of my life, meditating—living fully and in the present. I had lived successfully in the world of words and imagination, married two writers, my career involved writing. Through Sheri's guidance I started to learn the way of feeling and being open, nonjudgmental, and listening to what people were really, behind their pride and fear and also behind mine. And it is a constant learning process, rich and rewarding. All my real meaning and the reason I am on this earth is becoming clear. All my projects are blooming as is my health and my life is more full and blessed than I could have ever dreamed possible."

I taught my workshop two evenings, a week apart. This gave people a chance to absorb the ideas and to try them out on their own. When the group met again, class members could share their experiences with each other and raise questions. I encouraged the class members to speak freely, sharing themselves and their situations with each other. I found that it was healthy for people to see that they were not alone and to feel the support that flowed between them. Often the group's strength and support helped others to truly open themselves up.

Julia says, "It was profoundly moving to see the assembled group from very different walks of life and backgrounds open up to each other and find their real selves coming through. I had never cried before strangers, actually rarely cried in my life—but in Sheri's classes the trust and truth and warmth brought out torrents of feeling and tears. Psychoanalysis had never touched the pent-up self as those evening classes did for me. And we were all moved magically toward our real places in the grand scheme of things. I've been led and taught and learned to listen more carefully to my own inner guidance through several other channels since then, but Sheri was the one who showed me the way because she is totally loving and selfless and I trusted her, quite rightly, and will always be grateful to her."

As mentioned before, when Julia attended my classes she was so beautiful and charming that I could not imagine the depth of her suffering. I am touched to know that my classes helped her so much. In all honesty, I give most of the credit to Julia herself. It was apparent to me that she was a woman of power and action. Whatever ideas she learned from me, it is she who put them to use in her life, thereby ending her suffering. By the way, Julia has an adobe home in New Mexico, another home in Spain, and "lots of new friends, and a great life!"

I hope that you can see how these ideas have worked for people—people just like yourself. There are many others whose stories follow suit. You can be one of them. The following material is devoted to teaching you the methods of self-healing that were taught in my classes. May they serve you as they have served others!

- 11 -

Introduction to the Five-Phase Healing Program

Over the years, as I tried to make my experience work for me, I developed a daily program. Through my own desire to maintain health and a positive outlook I found myself compelled to put time aside every day to work with my own energy. After working with the meditation technique that will be outlined for you in Phase One of this program, I discovered a natural progression toward working with breath, hands, visualization, and belief systems. These make up the other phases of the program, all of which work interchangeably.

This program involves simple methods. Not only can they help combat illness and disease, but if you adopt them as a regimen, they may serve to strengthen and improve your current good health.

All the aspects of this program work together. For example, while you are working with your hands, you will be using visualization. Meditation and deep breathing will be used throughout all the phases. Therefore, although you may choose to concentrate on one particular phase of the program, you will be working with at least two or more of the phases at the same time. One phase strengthens the effectiveness of the other, and after a while it becomes very natural to flow back and forth through the phases. This is one of the reasons why the Five-Phase Healing Program works effectively and is easily fit into one's daily life.

One of the most important aspects of the healing program is that it focuses on an internal study of yourself and your belief systems. Phase Three will add a dimension to your meditation that will help you to discover what your beliefs are. This is vitally important to understanding yourself and your life. You will learn how to create new belief structures where necessary and how to assimilate them into your thinking.

Another aspect of the Five-Phase Healing Program that makes it unique and usable by anyone is its lack of reliance on any outside agents. All that you need to make it work is yourself and your willingness. Your breath is your own. Your beliefs, hands, symptoms, and ability to meditate stem from yourself also. You do not need to travel to any destination or spend any amount of money to use the abilities that exist within you now. If you can put aside twenty minutes a day for working with the Five-Phase Healing Program, you will find that in time it will work for you.

- 12 -

Phase One: Meditation

The first step in the program is the meditation technique. It will pave the way for greater receptivity to the exercises that follow.

Meditation induces relaxation. It slows down thinking patterns, which automatically relaxes the psyche. Studies conducted at the Harvard Medical School prove that meditation, when practiced consistently, lowers blood pressure and heart rates in hypertensive patients. I find that it helps me to center and focus my energy. More importantly, in the meditative state I am able to detach myself from my thoughts. In the meditative state I am able to perceive my ideas from a less biased, more passive perspective. In this way I gain insight into my life.

Although there are different meditation techniques, I am strongly in favor of the one I will outline for you here. Aside from the fact that this technique works, I am primarily interested in it because it focuses on breath, something that is internal and intrinsic to each of us. Of its own accord, breath has enormous value to the overall health of our bodies and minds and increases the benefits of the meditation technique. It is a well-known fact that every cell in our body requires oxygen. Through breath we are given life, and when we cease to breathe our physical existence is over. I was not aware of the shallow nature of my own breathing until I began to meditate. At that time I came to see how many actions I performed on one breath and how many words I would say before coming up for air.

127

Because we breathe automatically, most of us have developed habitual ways of breathing. Often these breathing patterns barely satisfy our needs and certainly do not fully nourish our bodies with the largest amount of oxygen possible. Is it any wonder then that many of us feel weak and tired or fall prey to illness? I would suggest to each of you that you observe your own breathing patterns. With the idea in mind that oxygen is the cells' food, consider whether your body is getting ample nourishment. Deep breathing alone can calm and increase your vitality.

When I am feeling tired or rundown, breath is a great rejuvenator. Try laying on your stomach. Place a pillow under your chest and abdominal area. I find that this position encourages breathing. When in need of a thorough breathing session, I lie in this position. Before I know it my breath begins to open up and I almost can't keep up with myself. I find that sometimes I have to open my mouth to allow for the maximum intake of oxygen. I usually emerge from this posture feeling energetic and refreshed.

Oftentimes, when a person suffers from a stomachache, he or she can be found rubbing the spot that hurts. It's only natural to want to reach into the troubled spot and somehow adjust the parts. Although our hands cannot physically do this, our breath can. Take a deep breath and observe. Your breath can enter and go deeply into your body. Take another breath and this time breathe in more deeply. Feel your breath reach down and enter your abdomen. In essence, your breath can internally massage your body from its entry at your nostrils to the pit of your stomach. In this way it can promote better functioning in the digestive, circulatory, and nervous systems. One of the best ways to develop deep breathing patterns is through meditation.

Find a comfortable place and put yourself in a comfortable position. I prefer the bath. The warm water is relaxing, and the bathtub is physically removed from the rest of the home. Some of my students have a particular easy chair that they use for meditation. Others find that a particular environment is very important and choose special surroundings for meditation such as the beach or the countryside. If you have easy access to such places, by all means make use of them. If you are living in the city, however, and cannot find a soothing environment, create one somewhere in your home. This can be done by selecting a place where you will not be disturbed. If necessary, turn on your telephone answering machine or take your phone off the hook for twenty minutes. You may enjoy lighting a candle or burning some incense, as I do. These small gestures indicate to your psyche that you are about to engage in something that you consider important.

Begin deep breathing, inhaling and exhaling through your nose. (Naturally, if you have a bad cold you will have to breathe through your mouth.) To amplify the sound of your breath, as well as block out other noises, it is helpful to place ear plugs in your ears. (Many drugstores sell wax ear plugs. They come in small round balls that will mold to fit the shape of your ear.)

Now as you inhale, think the sound *so*, and as you exhale, think the sound *hom*. *Sohom. Sohom.* Try it again. Inhale and think *soooooooooo*, and as you exhale hear the sound *hom*. Do it again. Notice how the sound *sohom* complements the sound of your breath. Listen . . . *sooo— hom*. Concentrate on the sound your breath makes. Try to hear it as a word. If it doesn't sound exactly like the word *sohom* to you, decide what it does sound like. Use another word if it rings truer for you, but hear the sound that your breath makes.

Eventually you may not feel the need to repeat any word or sound in your mind, for the sound of your breath may become very apparent in itself. Then you can focus solely on the sound of the breathing. However, to begin with I recommend repeating the word in your head. After a while the word will strongly reinforce the sound of your breath, which at first may seem difficult to hear and focus upon.

If you practice this, you will feel your body relax as you use the sound of your breath as a focus to remove your mind from your usual daily thoughts. As a matter of fact you may find it quite astonishing for as your thought patterns slow down, your entire system relaxes. Many students report that they become so relaxed that they often fall asleep. Therefore, they purposely sit up rather than lie down, to prevent this.

While meditating on your breath, you will most likely discover that your mind wanders. Welcome to the club! That's very natural. You may observe that your body tightens up if you think a thought that is unpleasant. That can show you the connection between mind and body. Sometimes it is better to follow a thought through than shut it off. However, as soon as you are able, focus your attention back on your breath. This is a good time to go back to repeating the word *sohom*, to help you refocus your attention on your breath.

Work with this meditation daily. It will help you to slow down the many thoughts that are racing through your mind. That in itself is relaxing. It can be of great benefit to your body and your spirit.

Beyond that, consider the fact that your own thoughts and feelings are forming your physical experience—thoughts that may have escaped your notice. As I mentioned earlier, from a meditative state you are in a better position to start observing what those thoughts and feelings are. While you are breathing and focusing on breath, you are able to take a step back from being directly inside your thoughts. From this vantage point you can view your thought processes as an observer. You are no longer at the mercy of rampant thoughts that you are unaware of, but an intimate observer to the way you think. You can begin to examine your thought processes, which is valuable beyond measure. The meditative state is the best place to view what's happening on your inner screen. Without going to therapy, you can gain clarity as to how you are forming the events in your life. This is the key if you desire change of any kind.

Later on we will look at how to analyze and work with the contents of our minds. At Phase One in this program, however, I am most interested in your development of the meditation technique. Use this as your starting point. Work first to achieve deep breathing, relaxation through your focus upon breath, and an intimate, close-up view of your own inner screen.

If you study meditation more thoroughly, you will find that it has been practiced in the East for centuries. The Hindus and Buddhists speak of surrendering the ego completely and merging with God and the universal forces.

While I am not saying that this is impossible, I have discovered that strong preconceptions about meditation often create frustration. People feel that they cannot achieve such lofty heights and give up the practice altogether. What I am offering is a tool. It has much value. Use it in your own way and it will accommodate to your individual needs.

The practice of meditation changes as it is used. There is no right or wrong way to experience this. Whatever comes up for you is exactly what you needed to take a look at. If you find, for example, that you become impatient, you will probably find that impatience is one of the issues that you deal with in your life. The same holds true for boredom or anger, so be open to however the experience flows for you, with the understanding whatever surfaces is an opportunity to learn.

I want to stress that you will only know the benefits of meditation through its practice. You can read books on the subject (there are plenty of them available), but that alone will not give you a practical, useful tool. Yet meditation is practical and useful and can be a life raft in the tumultuous sea of your thoughts. As you focus on breath and draw your attention away from your thoughts, you slow them down. The seas of your mind become calmer. You can begin to center yourself.

I therefore recommend practicing meditation on a daily basis, or as often as you can manage to work it into your schedule. I find meditation is most effective first thing in the morning. Some of my students meditate in the evening before going to sleep. "It ensures peaceful dreams and a better night's sleep," one told me. Naturally you have to work this into what may already be a very tight schedule. Therefore, use whatever time works best for you. With a pair of ear plugs, you may find that you are able to meditate on the train for fifteen minutes on the way to work! That's what I call meditation in action! However and whenever you do this, I think you will find it more than worthwhile. I wonder how I ever got along without it!

- 13 -

Phase Two: Characterized Breathing

Characterized breathing is a technique of deep breathing. Taught by Harry Edwards, it provides a method to enrich health by consciously absorbing cosmic energy.

Characterized breathing combines belief and visualization with a full breathing exercise. The results can be astounding. In the words of Harry Edwards, "We live in a 'sea' of cosmic force or energy." Although it is difficult to perceive, on a daily basis we unconsciously absorb this energy into our systems. In the way that a tree absorbs energy from solar rays, we absorb energy from the many forces that eddy about us. Through the use of characterized breathing we can consciously absorb this energy.

After eighteen years, I can attest to the fact that this method is beneficial in numerous ways. It increases vitality and mobilizes the body's innate healing forces. It helps to focus attention and to direct energy, providing a constant source of stability and rest. I use it at various times throughout the day. The experience of fear or of an unpleasant symptom automatically prompts me into using characterized breathing.

I go out of my way to use this method in order to energize myself. Harry claimed that it is the feeling of "knowing" that opens up the channels of receptivity to this energy. The belief that cosmic energy exists and that you can indeed draw it into you allows for the greatest utilization of this exercise.

It is my recommendation that you practice characterized

breathing on a daily basis. In a short time you will experience the beneficial results. Here's how to do it.

Step One: Relax through simple meditation. Begin with the same meditation technique that was used in Chapter 12. Focus on the sound *sohom*, the sound that your breath makes, and allow your mind and body to relax.

Step Two: Visualize and sense energy entering into you as you inhale. Continue your deep breathing and begin to visualize energy entering into you as you inhale. See streams of energy flowing into your nostrils as you draw breath into your body. Sense that you are taking in healing energy and power. Feel a refreshing, cool effect as the air travels through the bronchial tubes into the lungs. Keep in mind that the breathing should be slow and gentle, with deep, thorough inhalations.

Step Three: Cleanse and purify your body as you exhale. As you exhale, see your body eliminating waste. See it being cleansed and purified. If you are congested, you can envision your bronchial tubes clogged with debris. As you exhale you can imagine your breath sweeping them clean. The exhalation should be slow, accompanied by a sense that you are cleansing your body. If you have pain or any other physical difficulty, imagine that it is being cleared away with the exhalation. Remember that the fuller the exhalation, the more space that will be provided for the next inhalation. As you exhale, think the word *empty*. It will help you to exhale thoroughly.

Step Four: Combine Steps Two and Three. Begin to develop a slow, constant rhythm between your inhaling and your exhaling. Slowly exhale and empty your lungs, then in turn slowly inhale and fill them again. Keep your visualization and sense of purpose in mind. As I inhale I mentally say, "I inhale the energy of the universe into me." As I exhale I think, "I exhale any stale, old, unwanted, unneeded debris from my body."

This exercise will develop into an important and central part of your healing program. You may at times feel the need to take some short breaths between the long, slow inhalations. This is fine. You should practice this exercise in whatever rhythm is most comfortable. The overall purpose of this exercise can be lost if you become too rigid about the way that you perform it. I suggest, therefore, that you let it fall into its own pattern. You will discover that in time this exercise becomes very natural. You will use it often.

Variation A: Direct the energy as you exhale. Proceed with inhaling in the usual fashion, drawing energy into yourself. As you exhale, envision that the energy is going anywhere in your body that you wish to see it go. If you are dealing with a physical difficulty, imagine the energy entering your body at that point, and in your mind see the energy inducing beneficial changes. You may see light entering your body and surrounding the area that you wish to be healed. You may see colors instead of light. You may envision this process however you wish. Exact and correct images of the physical problem are not important, only the sense that energy is being directed to heal the problem. You are free to construct whatever images you want to as long as they support the healing purpose.

Variation B: Relax completely as you exhale. As always, draw energy into you as you inhale. This time as you exhale imagine all tension and stress being eliminated from your body. Feel yourself relax as you repeat this process. Starting at your toes and moving slowly up to your head, envision all tension being released as you exhale fully.

One of my students told a story in class about how he used this exercise to help him relax at an audition. He was waiting to read for a part. He felt nervous and very "uncentered." He remembered this exercise and decided to give it a try. He began to inhale, envisioning that he was drawing calm ocean breezes into him. As he exhaled he imagined every cell in his body closing its eyes and going to sleep. He repeated this visualization, he was not sure for how long. All of a sudden he looked around the room and realized that he had mentally stepped outside of the situation. He felt calmer and realized, at the same time, that his life was about more than the audition. This realization calmed him down more completely. He was very proud of himself. "For the first time," he said, "I felt that I was able to gain some control over my physical sensations of nervousness and my emotions!" By the time he was called to read for the part he was calmer and more in control than he had ever been at an audition before. As a result of his relaxation and subsequent poise, he gave an excellent reading. It certainly paid off because he got the part.

Characterized breathing is very effective in relieving pain. If I have pain of any kind, I imagine that I am drawing healing energy into me as I inhale. As I exhale, I envision the energy entering into my body at the place that hurts.

These are but a few of the ways that characterized breathing can be useful. As you work with it yourself you will create your own variations that put it to work for you!

- 14 -

Phase Three: Working with Beliefs

I cannot stress strongly enough the importance of working with beliefs. It is the supporting foundation to all other aspects of healing.

As I stated earlier, your beliefs create the reality that you experience. Your beliefs are your thoughts, backed up by your emotions. What you believe, expect, and focus on will be, in one way or another, woven into the fabric of your experience. Again this doesn't mean that you make a conscious decision to suffer. It does mean that your own energy is involved in creating your experience.

Our thoughts escape our notice. We think of so many things at once that often we are completely unaware of the nature of our ideas. We take them for granted. We don't even question them. Some of our ideas are faulty, limiting, and destructive, yet habit keeps us from seeing this. Without being aware of it, you can believe that you are unworthy, incapable, or bad. In one way or another most people can tell you why they are not good enough. They're not tall enough, rich enough, smart enough, affectionate enough, direct enough, indirect enough. The list goes on and on.

In my work I have observed that practically everyone believes that they know something about themselves that proves, beyond a shadow of a doubt, that they are not good enough. I've listened as people, obviously in great pain, shared with me the horrible secret that weighed so heavily on their heart. It never ceased to amaze me how insignificant these great sins were! Nothing I ever heard sounded so

136

terrible. To each and every person, however, this fault, this aspect of their humanity, was horrifying. They could not see the insignificance of their belief, because it substantiated a deeper-seated belief—such as that they were not good enough, they were evil, or they were insignificant. No greater pain exists than the unwillingness to love and approve of yourself. Self-approval is essential to health and emotional satisfaction.

It is important to understand that thoughts can effect changes in physical reality. Our thoughts make impressions upon reality that we then experience. Although you may be unaware of it, you are creating your experience at this very moment.

If you can accept the notion that your beliefs are responsible for your reality, then you have no other course of action, if you seek change of any kind, but to examine your beliefs. That involves taking the time to really listen to what your thoughts are.

If you are truly honest, you will find your own beliefs behind all the issues you hassle about. You will see why you feel as you do and will gain a far greater understanding of yourself and of the events in your life. You will begin to make connections between the ways you think and the situations you find yourself in.

It is helpful to keep in mind that just recognizing something as a belief doesn't always mean that—presto!—the belief is gone and all its ramifications with it. Usually some effort and time is required to change belief systems. The point is, however, that it can be done. At the very least modification is possible, in which case you might experience a lightening of your load, or a sense of breathing space.

Whatever your experience may be, unless you are sublimely happy, you can only benefit from an understanding of your beliefs. This lets you know who you are, what you think, and why you react and feel as you do. Without this understanding, life will seem like a series of mysteries. The positive and negative aspects of your life will seem to be thrust upon you from some unknown source and you will feel powerless to change or direct them.

Look at your beliefs! See what they are telling you! Are

they worth the price you may be paying for them? Could you, for just five minutes, see them in another light?

Ask yourself these questions about any beliefs you hold that say you're not good enough, capable enough, or worthy. Combat any ideas that make you unhappy. Stand up to limiting beliefs, be unwilling to accept them. You have the right to decide what you want to believe. You can absorb chosen beliefs into your psyche. Even if they seem impractical and completely beyond you, start believing them!

I have said over and over again in my classes that too much realism is sheer idiocy, too much reasonableness a waste of time. It may seem realistic to you to believe that you are inadequate in a certain area, but that so-called realism is helping to preserve that apparent inadequacy. As long as you believe it, it becomes the reality that you will experience. If your belief is limiting and making you unhappy, realistic as it may appear, it is not practical for you to believe it any longer.

Working with beliefs is essential. All the other forces around us relate to us in accordance with our beliefs. Of course there are healers that can help us, as I was helped by Harry Edwards. But imagine how much greater the power can be if you begin to address the mental and emotional reasons for your problems. I was fortunate, for unconsciously I had changed a good deal of the situations in my life that aggravated my fears. Therefore, I was open to the healing energy. But this is not always the case. There are people who are treated by numerous healers and whose conditions are not improved. These people, for whatever reason, are not open to the healing energy. They are blocking its effects. Maybe they don't feel worthy and deserving of life's benefits, one of which is health. Maybe they feel so unsafe that they cannot relax enough to let their energy flow. How can illnesses ever be overcome under such conditions? Disease can maintain disease no matter who the healer is. On the other hand, by working through your beliefs, you may discover that you have the power to create the change necessary to heal yourself without any outside help at all.

Phase Three of the Five-Phase Healing Program outlines a method for discovering your beliefs and altering them. Keep a pen and paper handy while doing this exercise. In this way you can jot down the beliefs you discover as the exercise unfolds. This list will be useful to you in numerous ways. Eventually you will have a handy list of beliefs you can refer to when needed.

Step One: Begin with the meditation described in Chapter 12. Focus your mind upon the sound of your breath. Feel you body and mind relax as you do so.

Step Two: Observe your daydreams and mental images. As you concentrate on your breathing, you will find thoughts, images, and daydreams forming in your head. Look at what you are thinking about. Observe the picture you are constructing in your mind. You are constantly writing scripts, so observe the script you are writing.

The key here is to maintain your awareness of breath. As you start to observe certain thoughts, you may find yourself becoming emotionally involved. As you mentally jump into the scenario, your breathing will tell you whether you are being drawn from an observant position into an emotional position. It will fluctuate, you will become less aware of it, and it will be almost impossible to hear the sound *sohom*. If, at this point, you can realign yourself with the sound *sohom* and return to consistent breathing, you will be able to step outside of your daydream into the observer's box. Now you can look at the daydream more clearly and understand what it is telling you.

Step Three: Determine the belief within your daydream. To do this, assume that the daydream is a script that you are writing. Ask yourself if this daydream were the plot in a play, what would the name of the play be? For example, if you imagine yourself loving someone who doesn't love you, the name of your play might be, *When I Love Someone, They Do Not Love Me Back*.

Step Four: Create the antidote suggestion. Once you have determined the name of the play, then you have your belief before you. If the belief is something like, "I have no difficulty in working out my problems," leave well enough alone. If, however, the belief is something like, "Whenever I love someone, he doesn't love me," it would be most advisable for you to create an antidote suggestion, opposite to the former one. In this case it would be something like, "I can find someone to love who will also love me."

Step Five: Apply the antidote suggestion. While still concentrating on breathing, maintaining an open and clear mind, repeat the antidote suggestion in your head. If it helps, you can envision the literal words in your mind. It is even more powerful to imagine a daydream that illustrates your new belief. Now if you would like to, allow yourself to step out of the observer's box and experience the satisfaction from the daydream as much as possible.

I hope you will use this exercise and allow yourself to really observe your own mind, thoughts, and images. Only then can you find the answers to the mysteries in your life. They are not really mysteries at all, but they will appear to be until you begin to make the connections between your thoughts and your experience. Once you can identify the beliefs that are ruling your life, you are in a position to start making changes—by consciously changing your thoughts and beliefs.

I want to remind you that if you discover your own methods for uncovering and changing belief systems, feel free to use them, and don't feel the need to change anything that is already working for you. If you find, however, that your beliefs are a puzzle to you, try the technique described in this chapter. It cannot be more simply put. Your daydreams, thoughts and images will show you what you believe. Take the time necessary to look within and you will give yourself the most effective tool for change imaginable. Know yourself and you will understand the nature of your experience.

I have been using this technique for years. Unconsciously I used it as a little girl, envisioning and dreaming what I wanted into my life. Now, on a daily basis I suggest to myself that my being is good, that my universe is safe, that my health will continue to flourish, and that these suggestions reach out to touch my loved ones as well. I experience greater contentment and satisfaction as a result. On a purely physical level, I have "worked with beliefs" to envision two wonderful children into my life and abundance in many forms. When seeking a publisher for this book, I used this technique daily. I identified my doubtful beliefs and mentally replaced them with positive antidote suggestions. I constructed daydreams in which I saw myself shaking hands, signing contracts, and seeing the title of my book written in bold letters on the front of countless books in bookstores throughout the country. If you are reading this now, then it certainly looks as though it worked!

I have students and friends who claim that they owe their success to working with beliefs. Teachers experience larger enrollment in their classes. Job offers pour in for actors and artists of all types. Love relationships come into being as well as much-needed affordable apartments. A number of my students are certain that their health situations improved as a result of working with their beliefs. Before you decide that you are locked into a certain situation, work with your beliefs. The power to change almost any situation rests in your hands!

I am not saying that this is effortless. On the one hand, this can be seen as playful daydreaming. On the other hand, observing your thoughts, admitting to doubts, fears and limiting beliefs, and consciously striving to change them takes definite work, willpower, and determination. Time has to be allotted. The same type of dedication needed to develop any skill or art may be called for. But then again, it is your life we're talking about. I can't think of a more worthwhile project to work on, can you?

- 15 -

Phase Four: Working with Hands

Healers have been working with their hands for centuries. Mothers lovingly rub sore spots on their children's bodies and perform healings all the time. I myself receive twice a month therapeutic massages.

Hands promote healing in many ways. Massage unblocks energy and stimulates circulation. Acupressure (the art of applying pressure to acupuncture points through the use of the hands alone) stimulates and redirects inner energy (the Chinese call this Chi). "The laying on of hands," healing in which hands are placed on or just above the body so energy can pass through them into the patient, is being taught to nurses at New York University.

An amazing use of hands in healing is practiced by psychic surgeons in the Philippines. As these healers touch or approach their patient, his or her body actually opens for them. It is said that in most cases the patient experiences no pain. Then the hands of the surgeon enter the body and perform whatever healing is necessary. Sometimes they will find a growth and remove it. After the procedure is completed, the surgical wound closes of its own, leaving no scar.

I have never been to the Philippines, nor have I witnessed this with my own eyes. I have seen films as well as read many books and articles on the subject. The healers claim to be guided by higher forces (as did Harry Edwards) that perform the surgeries through them.

In the case of the psychic surgeons, the elegance of their technique is less significant than their belief in the cooperation of energy forces around and within them. Many of them attribute the great miracles that take place through their work to God. Most state that their work is not done on a conscious level, and that they do not necessarily rely on their knowledge of the physical body. It is difficult for Westerners to accept such claims without viewing the events with their own eyes—and even then may doubt their experience. Rational explanations are always sought. In *The Heart of Healing*, Bruce and Jenny Wright Davis recount their journey to the Philippines to observe and study with some of these healing surgeons. They write about the strong faith and belief that guides these healers in their work. It is a truly fascinating area of healing that warrants further exploration.

If, theoretically, we accept that nonphysical energy exists and can be directed, then why limit its uses? True, the claims about psychic surgery seem more farfetched than other forms of healing. They work, however, with the same principles: matter is manipulated through energy. Is it less strange that energy came to me as a result of Harry Edward's efforts in England?

Physical life is full of amazing phenomena that I would have at one time considered impossible. Closing your mind to any of them makes the pool of life shallow, and denies access to valuable help.

Step One: Start by using the meditation technique in Chapter 12, focusing on your breath.

Step Two: Move into characterized breathing, envisioning energy coming into you as you inhale, and cleansing and purifying your body as you exhale.

Step Three: Continue with your characterized breathing but as you exhale envision the energy flowing into your hands. Use whatever images work best for you, but see the energy you inhaled flowing into your hands as you exhale. You may use the image of light flowing into your hands. I prefer the color red because it has a warm feeling to me. I envision the warm red healing energy entering my hands as I exhale. I imagine my hands becoming red as well.

Step Four: Place your hands where relief is needed. Continue with your breathing. As you exhale, envision the energy going through your hands and into the body. Use whatever images work for you, but see this being done. I envision the red healing energy that now flows through my hands, permeating the body and surrounding the area in need of healing. I imagine beneficial changes taking place.

You may discover after a while that your hands become very warm. This is a sign that the energy is indeed flowing into them. As with most things, the more you practice this, the more proficient you will become. If you are working with another person and are not quite sure where to place your hands, breathe in deeply and ask your inner self to guide you. In many cases you will instinctively sense where to place your hands. Go with your feelings in these matters.

To some, hands-on healing is a matter of faith. In the Philippines the healers are deeply religious, attributing miracles they claim no conscious understanding of to God. Harry Edwards, in *Thirty Years a Spiritual Healer*, states that during the war, healings were taking place all around him and he had no idea as to why. He didn't understand that he was a healer or what a healer was. He didn't try to develop healing abilities. As if prearranged, Harry became a healer to serve a power that, he discovered, flowed through him.

Some experts will deny any value to the laying on of hands while they accept the benefits of positive thinking.

I put the theories together. If we are energy, and the universe is also energy, then there is nothing preventing the interaction of energy forces—except maybe our own beliefs. Understanding that there are forces of energy around and within us, enables us to draw upon that energy. We can then direct it through our hands. Recognize that your own beliefs will determine just how much energy you will allow yourself access to. Continue to work, therefore, with your belief systems. Thus you will not allow your doubts to prevent you from utilizing this energy. As I inhale I think the words, "I inhale the energy of the universe into me." As I exhale I think, "The energy is entering my hands and flowing from my hands, into the body." Statements of this type can help you to direct your thought energy to work for you.

I have experienced many positive results with hands-on healing. I am sure that many of you will find that the ability to transfer your own loving energy is not a gift reserved for the gods alone. Harry Edwards wrote that the most important qualification for healership was the desire to see people relieved of their suffering. If you naturally have that inclination, then there is a healer brewing inside of you that can begin to emerge if you so desire. The next time you are not feeling so well, or someone close to you complains of an ailment, place your hands on the area that warrants attention and begin your breathing and visualizing. Try to incorporate the belief that healing is possible and ask the forces around you to assist you in your goal. You may become very excited to discover that energy is indeed available to you. With practice you will become more comfortable using your hands for healing.

Many of my students are using hands-on healing regularly with themselves, friends, and loved ones. Interestingly, many of them report success with their pets. It has been discovered that animals are loving, compassionate, and respond dramatically to the healing effort. Therefore, do not forget to include them in your healing work. You may find that they are more open to it than some of the people you know!

16

Phase Five: Visualization

Whenever I feel a symptom coming on, from a headache to a stomachache, I can greatly relieve it by using characterized breathing. Combined with visualizations, characterized breathing becomes even more useful. In Phase Five of this healing program, you create a visualization that relates specifically to the symptom in question. Through imagery you envision the symptom being overcome.

The use of visualization is so effective that people are incorporating it into their lives for many purposes. It can be used to create change in any area, but for now I will limit the discussion to health.

Everyone can relate to examples of their bodies and minds working together. Think of the way your body becomes aroused if you look at erotic films and photographs, or of the way your heart beats quickly when you are frightened. Your body immediately reacts to your thoughts. We have seen, through biofeedback research, that we possess the ability to control certain bodily functions mentally. For example, people are learning to raise and lower their body temperature as well as their heart rates at will.

If you accept this mind-body connection, then imagine the power at your disposal if you replace negative imagery with strong powerful images that support your purpose. Consider a person who has a cancerous tumor. The person imagines it frequently: its size, its shape, and its destructive potential. The person, in turn, becomes fearful. Her heart rate most likely increases. As her anxiety grows, her mind finds its way back to the original image of the tumor. This naturally increases the power behind and within the growth itself. All in all, this person has increased the strength of the condition while her own innate healing abilities have been ignored and therefore weakened.

Now let's turn the coin over and see how this person can make imagery work *for* her. First she relaxes through the use of meditation. Then she uses characterized breathing to absorb and direct her energy more completely. Next she selects the image of a snowball to represent her tumor. As she inhales she envisions healing energy flowing into her. As she exhales she envisions that energy going directly to the snowball and melting it. At first she may see the snowball getting smaller, but by the time she completes the exercise, she doesn't see the tumor at all. It has been dissolved. Through imagery, she has mobilized her body against her illness.

Step One: Relax through simple meditation. Follow the meditation technique outlined in Chapter 12. Slowly inhale and exhale, focusing on the sound your breath makes. Allow your body to relax as you focus your mind on the sound of your breath.

Step Two: Add characterized breathing to the meditation technique. As you inhale, feel that you are absorbing healing energy into you. As you exhale, mentally direct your energy to the afflicted part of your body. This will allow for greater absorption and direction of energy.

Step Three: Create a mental image of your symptom. While continuing to breathe deeply, inhaling energy, experience the symptom. As you do so, create an appropriate image for it. For example, if you have back pain, you might imagine a fire burning in your back. If you have a headache, you might envision a huge knot inside your head.

Step Four: Create the antidote image, the image that contradicts the image of your symptom. For example, if you envisioned back pain as a fire burning in your back, your antidote image will be of pouring water over the fire and extinguishing it. If for a headache, you envisioned a knot inside of your head, your antidote image will be undoing the knot until it is completely untied.

Step Five: Concentrate on your antidote image. For at least ten minutes while breathing and absorbing energy into you, visualize your antidote image. As clearly and vividly as possible, using whatever image works best for you, maintain the picture of your antidote image. See the problem being solved through imagery.

You may be pleasantly surprised to see how remarkable the results of working with visualizations are. I personally find them incredibly useful. I want to remind you, however, that your beliefs are also very powerful. You may be visualizing wonderful things happening to you, while at the same time you believe that you don't deserve them, or that you are not capable of achieving them. Because one idea can easily neutralize the other, it is essential to understand your belief systems and to work to alter any beliefs that limit your ability to use these healing techniques.

Careful attention to the details of your visualizations can give you a deeper understanding of your beliefs. The way that you envision certain situations can be a great clue to the way you feel about them. In turn, visualizing those beliefs you want to establish will introduce them into your psyche. Visualization in and of itself is a very powerful tool. Combined with belief work, it becomes astounding. Too often we visualize our fears and negative beliefs, not realizing that we are helping to weave them into the fabric of our existence, not believing that we have the power to create the results we desire.

Therefore I cannot stress enough the necessity of observing, understanding, and altering your beliefs. At the same time, you are free to create visualizations to work with any situation you wish. The visualizations need not be sophisticated. You can create as playful and childlike a visualization as you want. The key here is to imagine the beneficial result you desire. Beyond that there is no rule.

For example, I have seen drawings produced by children with cancer who were undergoing chemotherapy. The illustrations show their medication as knights in shining armor attacking the "bad cells." The fact that these drawings are not necessarily clinically correct is not important. The idea is what matters. The same holds true for any visualization.

It is the overall idea and outcome that counts, and not the manner in which it is demonstrated.

It is important to remember that your symptoms are telling you that something is wrong in your body. Hence, something is disturbed in your emotional and mental system. These disturbances stem from your beliefs; however, you are not at the mercy of them. You can sort through them, come to understand them, and change them for the better.

Each of us is an integral part of our world. Through our beliefs, attitudes, and feelings we impact upon it in numerous ways. As a result of our ignorance the planet suffers its own symptoms. We simply cannot ignore this.

If our world is going to continue to grow, someday reaching a point of greater humanity, it will be because we have chosen to continue to evolve. That evolution is happening now! It is happening to you and to me and to countless others who are choosing to see themselves as creators of their world. People are choosing to harness the great power of their thoughts and let go of outmoded limiting ideas. That's evolution, and the earth feels that evolution! When just one person chooses to walk beyond his or her negative beliefs and fears, thereby setting his or herself free, that freedom is felt throughout the earth! It has been said that that energy is powerful enough to hold a fault line together. *Just think of that!* Imagine the extra added power when many of us take the time to send joyous positive energy outward to the world in which we live!

Again, I believe we need to work from the inside out. We must change our own individual beliefs before we can expect to change the world. But as we change, the world changes.

Guide Visualization

Another valuable way to use visualization is through guide images. Although it is my belief that we already contain the answers to our own questions, often people are reluctant to accept this. Therefore, although they may receive strong impulses to take a certain action, or an answer to one of their questions may pop into their mind, many people are unwilling to trust and utilize the information. Yet if this same information were given to them by a psychic or a wiseman they would feel no hesitation. Therefore, it can be very helpful to visualize a guide or teacher image through which you can communicate with your inner self.

I have used this method extensively in my classes. Many of my students have found it to be extremely helpful as well as lots of fun. Some students see old sages who answer their questions clearly and concisely. Others have reported seeing gnomes, elves, whales, and land animals. One of my students was surprised to see his best friend appear to him.

It's interesting that the guides that come to mind reflect the beliefs and attitudes of the person. People who believe that their guide should be serious usually see serious images, while those who tend to see the matter more playfully envision playful guides. Some people believe that they can not contact a guide at all and as a result have more difficulty doing so. However, with a little effort, most people find that they can indeed visualize a guide to converse with. Let's look at how to do this:

Step One: Begin by using the meditation technique. Feel your body relax as you concentrate on the sound of your breath.

Step Two: Begin characterized breathing to absorb extra energy into you. As you exhale, feel your body relax more fully as you let go of your thoughts and everyday cares.

Step Three: Visualize a place where you feel relaxed and at peace. You can imagine that you are sitting on a beach or on a mountaintop. Choose whatever surroundings give you a feeling of peace and serenity.

Step Four: Envision a guide walking toward you. This guide can be male, female, or animal. See the guide as clearly as you can. If nothing comes to mind immediately, continue with your breathing and suggest to yourself that soon a guide will appear. In most cases, a guide image will come to mind. Accept this image as your own. Do not judge it. You may think that it is silly or childlike but this doesn't matter. You can still receive valuable information through your guide, so keep an open mind.

Step Five: Ask your guide the questions that are on your

mind. Listen to the answers you receive and be willing to accept them; they spring from your inner self and undoubtedly have meaning. Some of my students report that the messages are incredibly applicable and meaningful to them. You may want to ask your guide its name and why it has appeared to you in this particular fashion. By all means thank your guide for coming.

You can call upon your guide anytime you need to. Many people have come to rely on guides as friends—friends that provide valuable insights and information. You will be amazed to discover the enormous storehouse of information you can tap into through this means. It is a pleasurable way to work with yourself as well.

I have been very impressed by the work of Dr. Martin L. Rossman. For over fifteen years Dr. Rossman has taught visualization techniques to thousands of patients and health professionals. His book *Healing Yourself* offers a wonderful program for healing yourself through imagery. (For further information, see references.)

Part IV

Part IV

17

Combination Acts; Some Additional Tips for Dealing with Symptoms, Tension, and Emotions

One morning, while doing my usual meditation routine, I was troubled with a slight tension headache. As I did my characterized breathing combined with hands-on healing, I began to gently press my forehead on the place that bothered me. As I inhaled I imagined myself drawing in energy. As I exhaled not only did I see the energy going through my hands, but I used my hands to apply physical pressure as well. After finding this to be very relieving, I began to experiment with other ways of combining breathing, visualizations, and physical acts—thus the term *combination acts* was born.

There are numerous ways in which combination acts can be applied to living. You can combine breathing and visualization with almost any physical act and use it to increase your effectiveness. I am sure that many of you, as you begin to work with this, will discover ways that never would have occurred to me. It's fun to discover new ways. I will list a few that are useful to me.

Using the hands for pressure. As described earlier, in the case of the tension headache, I find the use of pressure, combined with breathing and visualization, very therapeutic. If I have a backache, headache, or plain old sore feet, I press and manipulate that portion of my body. As I inhale I envision drawing in energy. As I exhale I envision that energy entering the area I am pressing. If my baby is unusually cranky, demanding that I carry him a good deal of the day, my right arm often becomes sore. I receive a lot of relief from just five minutes of pressing my arm between my thumb and second finger. I slide them down my arm, moving over the parts that hurt. At the same time I maintain my breathing and visualizing. When you combine your breath and your mind with a physical act, you help to increase the effectiveness of the effort. Your thoughts and healing energy become aligned with the motion of your physical body. This intensifies the energy within the motion.

I feel fortunate in having discovered Carolyn Bengston, my massage therapist. Carolyn has a deep knowledge of inner energy and does not merely give me a routine rubdown. She is definitely aware of the nonphysical energy she directs into me, energy that extends beyond her physical touch. I can sense, as she centers herself through breath, her intention to direct her own energy into me, through the medium of touch. Although massage in itself is physical, Carolyn and I are both aware of an energy exchange between us that is not physical at all.

Working with water. Water, as I've mentioned, is an extremely useful and therapeutic tool for healing. A woman recently told me she only takes showers because she can't imagine sitting in the bath with nothing to do. Some of the therapeutic value in bathing rests in the very fact that you are removed and induced to relax. Beyond that, water, in its many forms, can be effectively used in combination acts. When I am taking a bath, I like to put my forehead under the faucet and let cool water gently run over it. This can be especially relieving for tension in your head. Of course I do this as a combination act with the usual breathing and visualization. I also find it very useful while standing in the shower. I move my body so that the water lands where I want it to. I maintain my breath and visualization to increase the effectiveness of the water pressure on my body. Water combination acts can soothe minor ailments and discomforts. Blocked energy can be freed and circulation increased.

When working with symptoms I employ water, ice, heat, pressure, massage, acupuncture, homeopathic remedies, Bach flower remedies, diet, herbal remedies, vitamins, healing salves, and medical tablets, potions, and salves. (For further information see appendix.) I leave nothing out. Anything helpful to you is welcome. As long as you don't rely on medicine in lieu of dealing with your inner self, feel free to take advantage of all the remedies at your disposal.

A shower can be therapeutic as well as rejuvenating. Ice can be incredibly useful in dealing with injuries. It has a numbing effect and prevents excessive swelling. It is the finest healing tool for burns that exists. It is also particularly soothing for headaches. Heat works wonders on sore muscles, backaches, stomachaches, and menstrual cramps. Acupressure and massage manipulate, stimulate, and help promote the body's innate healing intelligence.

As you know, tension can wreak all kinds of havoc upon the human body. It can attack an organ or stiffen a joint. When I discover that a part of my body is sore and aching, the first thing I do is to favor that part of my body. I try to use it less, resting it as much as possible. In essence I baby that part of my body. As an animal lovingly licks its wounds, I begin to massage or apply hot or cold compresses to the troubled area. Along with this, I try to ascertain the particular cause of the problem. In many cases, a sore arm is the result of a stiff stance, unconsciously assumed as a result of tension. I therefore make a conscious effort to relax the arm, allowing it to go limp. Naturally, working with the meditation technique helps to induce a state of mental relaxation, which is necessary to help us relax our bodies. Usually, if I follow this formula, by the next morning the symptom subsides. If not addressed, the symptom increases in strength. Over a period of time it can easily develop into a chronic problem. It is therefore wise to attend to symptoms at their onset, nipping them in the bud, so to speak.

Our thoughts, feelings, emotions, and bodies are one connected system. They cannot be separated, nor can the effect they have upon each other be denied. Our thoughts and our feelings stem from our beliefs. As you work with your beliefs, you will be able to understand your thoughts and emotions far more clearly. Phase Three of the Five-Phase Healing Program will give you a handy tool for discovering what some of your beliefs are. Let's look at other ways of understanding our thoughts and emotions and dealing with them.

In simple terms talk to yourself. Ask yourself why you are afraid or depressed and write down the answers that come to mind. Be open to the answers that you receive. Keep in mind that you do not have to accept destructive attitudes forever. For example, you may realize that you are afraid of loving because you have been hurt. At the same time you can realize that although that attitude may have prevented you from accepting love, you will not accept that attitude any longer. Again, talk to yourself. Say, "I will not accept this attitude any longer!" In this way you are declaring a new set of beliefs, standing up to and weakening the old ones.

The same holds true for depression. Obviously depression can create all manner of symptoms ranging from lethargy to chronic physical problems. And yet you do not simply fall into a depression. Your beliefs are most certainly involved in it.

In this case, rather than running from the depression, face it. Follow the feelings through and ask yourself why you feel this way. If you study your thoughts honestly and closely, you will uncover the roots of your depression.

It is also important to learn to express your emotions. If you feel unable to do this, you will dam them up inside yourself. Eventually they will come out—often in the form of physical symptoms. There is no point in denying any of your emotions, or of suppressing them. By allowing them to flow they will pass and change in the same way that the weather does. On the other hand, if you hold them inside there is no motion. The emotions become increasingly more volatile over time and the situation more difficult to change. Even if you just begin to talk about your feelings to a friend, you will relieve some of the pressure.

Take, for example, the case of a woman who came to see me for counseling. She was a kind and gentle woman in her forties. She had been suffering from multiple physical conditions for many years. Shortness of breath, allergies to many different substances, and claustrophobia were only a few of her many difficulties. After we spoke for some time it became apparent that she was riddled by guilt over a childhood experience. Having been raped by her stepfather, she was convinced that she was evil and responsible for the event. For years she walked around holding her guilt over this experience inside, quite literally making herself sick over it. After gathering the bravery to finally admit this to me, she broke down. The tears that flowed from her once-guarded emotions finally were allowed release. I remember holding her and comforting her, trying desperately to make her understand that she was not to blame.

Her physical conditions did not clear up overnight. We met quite a few more times and spoke over the phone. Gradually she came to understand that she was merely a child when this event took place and not the guilty party. Slowly she began to come out of her shell by attending some of my classes and interacting socially. The last time we had contact she called to say that she was moving out of the city, something that she had desired for a long time. She was writing music, was involved in a happy relationship, and was only minimally bothered by one remaining symptom.

I am certain that expressing her guilt allowed it to finally flow out of her. As a result her bodily symptoms were able to ease up while her life became more full and satisfying.

Allow your feelings their expression. Let them go and you will most assuredly take the pressure off. At the same time work to change limiting beliefs. Your beliefs are not necessarily a true picture of reality. Feel them, express them, but work to change those that are not creating the results that you desire.

- 18 -

Working with Physicians

I realize that after reading this book up to this point, you may feel confused as to how to integrate the program and my suggestions into your personal life. Should you stop going to medical doctors and taking prescribed medication? Should you alter your diet radically? Should you move to a monastery where you need only meditate and can avoid the pressures of living? Obviously, you can choose to do anything you want. I, however, prefer to maintain a common-sense attitude and choose from all the ideas presented those that work best for me.

As for doctors, as long as you realize that your state of health is basically your responsibility, then you would be foolish to refuse the benefit of their knowledge. When I was recovering from my ileostomy, I bitterly detested medical doctors. I was angry that they hadn't been able to come up with an easier solution to my problems, and I was appalled by the amount of pain involved in healing from the outside in. When I was healed from my serious, possibly fatal liver disease, I faulted doctors for their lack of knowledge concerning spiritual healing. It irritated me that they considered themselves authorities on health when they understood nothing about the forces that restored mine. Actually, I blamed doctors for everything that happened to me. I was fond of saying that I would never allow myself to be treated medically again.

I felt that since the cause of illness was rooted within one's own psyche, taking medication only confused the body intelligence with a third element. The body now had to deal with the symptom, its cause, *and* the medication. It seemed to me that clouding the symptoms would never lead one to discover the reasons for an illness. Even if some relief was achieved, it could easily be short-lived. In my case the illness was fed by such enormous fears that it had far more power than any drug I took. Doctors and medicine seemed pointless to me.

I now see these ideas as quite distorted. It is we who have given our doctors the awesome responsibility for our health. Often we know or do very little to ensure it on our own. Many of us have no idea about who we are, what our beliefs are, and how we are using our energy. We go through life maintaining judgmental, limiting ideas about ourselves, and then go crying to our doctors when we begin to experience a symptom. We are all the more shocked and appalled if our doctors do not present us with an immediate remedy to get us out of the mess we have gotten ourselves into.

Norman Cousins, in *Anatomy of an Illness* and *The Healing Heart,* formulates the essential elements for maintaining health. He mentions positive emotions, hope, faith, love, laughter, and the will to live as important factors. If you look more closely at these factors, you will see that they are intimately connected to his beliefs.

From reading his books I found Norman Cousins to be a man who possessed an abundance of positive beliefs. He displayed great confidence and faith in himself, and a healthy sense of humor as well as intelligence. Despite a frightening illness, he was not afraid to express his views to his medical doctors, who in turn gave his ideas consideration. This is a very unusual doctor–patient relationship. Mr. Cousins was actually involved in the decision making process concerning his treatment.

I was impressed by his analysis of his state of mind prior to becoming ill. He realized that his life-style had become too stressful. He had not been allowing himself the necessary time to relax and enjoy himself, thus stunting the happy emotions that serve to create health. He therefore began to add laughter to his treatment by watching funny movies and tapes of *Candid Camera* shows. He discovered that laughter actually relieved his pain.

Through combining his own common sense and intelligence with the advice of his doctors, Norman Cousins was successful in overcoming two very serious bouts with illness. Unfortunately the average patient does not usually follow suit. Faced with a serious illness most people react emotionally rather than rationally. Panic sets in, and the patient's worst fears and beliefs rise to the surface, accompanied by a sense of helplessness. At this point the doctor takes over, doing whatever he feels is best for the patient, while the patient absolves himself of all responsibility. In many cases, the patient's lack of understanding leads him to make no effort to change or alter the life-styles or beliefs that caused the illness. The doctor and the patient may soon be fighting a losing battle.

I certainly believe that our emotions determine the state of our energy, which in turn determines the state of our health. Sometimes we need a life-style change, other times we need a change of attitude. The point, however, is that the responsibility is our own and cannot be handled for us. To blame doctors because your body is failing you is not only unfair to them but to yourself; for in this way you do not recognize your own power to make the changes necessary to heal. To decide to reject medical help altogether is equally foolhardy. Medication can and has in many cases brought about positive changes. Surgeons have saved countless lives, and whether you like it or not, so has chemotherapy.

I think that it is best to maintain a commonsense attitude toward our health, making use of all the tools at our disposal. Harry Edwards always said that ideally, spiritual healing and medical science should work hand in hand. After all, they are both trying to achieve the same result: the healing of the sick. Doctors can tell us many things about the state of our bodies, while spirit and thought energy can be applied to promote inner changes. Antibiotics can be given to help overcome infections, while the individual involved can work along with his own mind, creating visualizations of overcoming the infection. This is often done with chemotherapy patients, who choose to work mentally along with the power of the medication rather than fight it.

In a larger sense, anything that helps you return your body to a state of health should be considered healing. I have no problem with taking a Tylenol tablet for a headache, although I do try, at the same time, to understand that the cause of the headache rests within myself, and that the headache is telling me something. I seek to understand what that something is, and to make the adjustments necessary to reverse the situation. As long as we are willing to do this, then there is no harm done if we seek relief through any number of means.

Without feeling that you have to change your life completely, work with the Five-Phase Healing Program. If you can make time to include this practice in your daily life, you will derive enough insight into your beliefs to start putting valuable changes into motion. Twenty to thirty minutes a day is not a lot of time. I have come to rely upon this program so very much that I wonder how I ever kept my life together before I developed it.

I would like to add that the maintenance of good health is antithetical to the perfection kick. We must understand, because we are growing and becoming, that there is always much to learn. Clearly, if we had all the answers, if there was nothing left to improve upon in ourselves, we would be perfect, but we would be statues, finished beyond change. Nothing can exist without change in a universe that is constantly changing, and so it is only natural that we grow into more tomorrow than we are today. Therefore, accept the little imperfections that you experience with your health, as well as with your life. Allow them to be okay with you, and you will discover more space to create the changes that you need. Don't berate yourself for taking an antibiotic or a headache tablet, but do seek to understand which of your own beliefs are creating every aspect of your health and your experience. Don't make the mistake of labeling doctors as the enemy, but seek to understand how your beliefs make an enemy of your own energy. I often say that it takes a lot of energy to make a headache—energy working against itself. By learning to take responsibility for that energy, you are in a better position to claim health, as well as employ the help of medical science and doctors.

The same applies when you seek help from psychic or spiritual healers. If you are unwilling to make some of the changes necessary within yourself, the energy directed to you may have little or no effect. Therefore, be open to changing beliefs and experiences that stand in the way of your achieving health. Give up your attachment to things being a certain way in your life, especially if your life depends on your doing so. Try to develop as healthy an attitude toward change as possible. Think of the tree whose branches bend in the wind. If held too rigidly, the branches will break. This could be the case with you. Imagine being as receptive to the healing energy of the universe as the earth is to the rain. You do not need to be certain about it, but work with your beliefs to be at least open to new possibilities.

- 19 -

The Pleasure Formula

How important is joy to the health of your body? How much healing can actually take place in the absence of happiness?

When the level of effort in people's lives completely overwhelms the level of pleasure, they begin to wonder what they are living for.

Some people believe that we must rise above physical reality and the material world. Others feel that physical life is all that there is, and we should grab what we can.

I believe in a mixture. We are more than our physical bodies and certainly life is more than physical pleasure and material acquisition. On the other hand, we are physical for a reason. That reason has more to do with experiencing our flesh in all of its ramifications than with rising above it. I don't believe in transcending an experience so varied and rich as physical reality.

Life is not about pleasure alone, but pleasure is important, and often overlooked. Certainly we all have goals and projects to accomplish, but what matters most isn't necessarily the speed with which they are completed, but the way we go about doing them. Are we able to appreciate the moment when they are taking place, or are we so goal-oriented that the moment completely eludes us? Do you ever find yourself so wrapped up in getting your life done that you don't even notice the sky or laugh at a joke? Isn't it true that once you have reached your goal, another goal takes its place?

Don't give up pursuing worthwhile goals, but take the time to see that your life is about more than goals. We must appreciate fully the experience of being alive. That will mean different things to different people, of course, but how many of us fritter our days away in what we think of as responsible action, never stopping to ask ourselves if this is all that our life is about, or if we even have the sense about us to taste the food that we gobble down for lunch.

It is sad that many of us are so totally wrapped up in our goals that we race down the road of life without taking the time to stop and smell the flowers. Our children grow up before our eyes. One generation dies to make room for another. After a while you begin to wonder what it is all for.

When people come to me who are ill and attempting to heal their bodies, I usually confront them with the idea that if their body is breaking down, it is definitely time for reevaluating and making some changes in what they are doing with their lives. If they have come to me, they are usually open-minded and ready for anything. The next thing that I do is ask them what it is that gives them pleasure, and often request that they make a list of such things. They usually come up with simple things like watching a good movie or eating an ice cream cone, having lunch with a friend, or reading a good book. Of course I then ask when the last time was that they indulged this pleasure, only to hear, all too often, that they just haven't had time lately. Having the time and making the time are two different things, I inform them. I then insist that each day they do at least one thing, however great or small, to ensure an experience of pleasure.

You may ask, can the experience of pleasure actually guarantee good health in our bodies? While I will not go so far as to say that anything guarantees anything, I certainly believe that pleasure promotes health, since it conjures up the positive healing emotions present within us. In the same way that sadness, disappointment, and stress can insidiously break down our health without our awareness, fun and joy can rebuild it. I recommend pleasure to all those who wish to maintain or regain health. From daily pleasure, to weekly pleasure, to monthly, and finally, accumulated yearly pleasure, remember that the moments of your existence are passing you by, never to pass this exact way again. Let the living experience of each of your days hold some joy for you, as it is precious, and it will most assuredly work to maintain your health, both mentally and physically.

It is also important to remember that even in situations of adversity, when it is not easy to experience pleasure, we have greater resources than we may presently know. We can learn to view our situations in ways that make them less painful, ways that even make them useful, or we can decide to give up trying altogether, and thus throw our lives away. I know that back in 1969, when I opened my eyes in the recovery room and Barry confirmed that the ileostomy had been performed, I had the choice to either give up and possibly die, or fight with all the strength at my disposal to regain my health and freedom. For me there was no choice, or rather something deep inside of me had already made the choice, for I knew at that moment that life, with all of its problems, was far too precious to throw away. As time passed, that truth became all the more apparent, and as I sit here now I am filled with enormous gratitude and joy for the life that I am leading.

When you find yourself in adversity, hold on to your dreams and aspirations and desires. Don't be so sure that the skies cannot brighten, or the terms of reality ever change. Try to gain some perspective on your current situation, knowing that your life is about more than that, and will be, if you don't give up on it. Remember to inject whatever small pleasures into your life that you can, for the effect will be cumulative and will lead you in the directions that you need to take. Joy should be a part of your living experience, and even if something prevents you from taking part in pleasurable activities, alternative pleasures are always waiting to be discovered.

The pleasure formula means this: make room in your life for the things that bring you pleasure, and you will be a more joyous person. You will have more exuberance for others and for life itself, and your work efforts will overwhelm you less. Your health will reflect the joy you experience, and when you look back on your life, you won't feel that it has passed you by but that you have lived it to the fullest and to the best of your abilities. You'll have a damn good time doing it, too!

- 20 -

Self-Love, Acceptance, and Forgiveness

Self-love. Acceptance. Forgiveness. Such easy words to write, not such easy ones to live by. Let's break them down and look at what they mean.

Self-love is a very important concept. How many of you feel ready and willing to love yourselves just as you are, even with all your so-called imperfections? How many of you love yourselves fully and completely with no holds barred?

I find most people further away from any real self-love than they realize. They have plenty of reasons to feel justified in not loving themselves fully. For example: they're too impatient, or get frustrated too easily; they're too fat or they're too thin; they're too old or they're too young. Whatever it is, it justifies denying themselves love. People do it all the time. They deny themselves love because they do not think that they are living up to the ideals they carry around in their minds. They berate themselves for what they are not.

An ideal is only an ideal. It may be alive in your mind, but it is not living. You, on the other hand, are alive and vulnerable, changing and growing, and, I'm sure, filled with the best of intentions. Some of you are tall and some of you are short, some of you are heavy while others of you are frail and thin, but you are all human beings, alive now as what you are, worthy of your own love and approval. Not only are you worthy of it but you need it, and your physical and mental health and happiness depend upon it. When you love your body, you automatically bless it in the most awesome and yet subtle ways. Such a level of energy may escape your awareness completely, but when you are willing to love your body, if for no other reason than it is the only one you've got, then that acceptance is somehow understood by your cells, and it protects your health. By not being in conflict with your body, you allow it to breathe and function. The same ideas apply to living. You cannot love life and hate yourself. You cannot completely love anything until you are able to love yourself, and your life will always be less than it can be until you can learn to appreciate yourself as yourself.

It does not do to say, "I love myself but," or "I will love myself when." There will always be but's and when's until the day you die. But if you can look at yourself and say, "I love myself for all that I am and all that I am not," then your life can be filled with challenges and changes that are not a drag, but a work of art. You can then allow yourself to be the self that you are, and not berate yourself for your mistakes and weaknesses. You can look at them, admit to them, and do what you can to change them, but you do not use them as reasons to deny yourself love. To deny yourself love is to pull the shades down and block out all the sun. Nothing can grow in such a gloomy environment, and certainly nothing can thrive. Your love and affirmation of yourself is the most important gift that you must give yourself if you have any designs on having a joyous life.

One of the more important keys to achieving self-love is acceptance. If you cannot accept what is, then you find yourself in a position where you are always in conflict. So much energy is then wasted in the conflict that there is little or nothing left over to create anything else.

EST trainers use the expression "what you resist persists," and I have seen this come true many times. In dealing with myself or with others, when I finally get to the point of saying, "So be it, if that is the best I'm going to get then it will just have to do," that's usually when the situation turns itself around and becomes more gratifying. That doesn't mean that if you find yourself overweight, you have to be thrilled about it. However, if you can relax, accept the reality of it without hating and berating yourself, then you are in a far better position to start changing your beliefs and living experience. Nothing can be achieved through rejection and hatred except more of the same.

Often I feel I am too impatient, and that I rush around too much. I recognize that beneath that impatience is the belief that if I don't hurry, I might not get it done and that by pressuring myself I am more likely to complete my goal. This is a faulty belief that I am working to change. At the same time I recognize that by accepting my impatience, seeing it as something that may not be my strongest point but then again is not my demise either, I allow myself to be who I am. I am not fighting myself or berating myself. As each day provides the opportunity for me to do better (sometimes I do, sometimes I don't), at least I can breathe and live my life. If you cannot accept what is and what you are, you cannot expect to do very well in the self-love department. You will always be fighting what you see as your faults. Being human, you're bound to have your share of them. Seth once said that we were not perfect, but that we were "perfectly ourselves." I remember that when I find I am being overly judgmental and hard on myself.

By learning to accept yourself and see yourself in a less critical light, you also learn to be less judgmental of others. In the same way that you are able to love yourself, even and despite all of those things that you see as your faults, so are you able to love others. They no longer have to be perfect in your eyes when you no longer have to be perfect in your eyes.

And when you get down to it, all of this has a lot to do with forgiving. Forgive yourself for not being perfect, for making mistakes, and quite frankly for being human! Not that we should need our own forgiveness, but it seems as though we do. We need to forgive rather than blame ourselves for not being perfect. Not because we possess the latent ability to be perfect someday, but just because we are what we are. We need to forgive others for what we see as their faults, not because they have the potential to do better, but because that is who they are right now. If we can do this, with ourselves and with others, we will find a lot more love and joy in our experience.

I am extremely emphatic about the importance of self-love, self-appreciation, acceptance of what is, and forgiveness for what is not. You can spend your time finding fault with yourself, your body, your life, and other people, but you will not accomplish much beyond creating dissatisfaction in your life. Nothing will ever be good enough for you, and you will wonder why others seem to enjoy life so much more than you do.

I sometimes ask people who feel that life is boring and worthless, and that they are undeserving and worthless, to consider the following situations. In the first one you imagine that tomorrow the world is going to end, and then ask yourself, assuming that this is your last day on earth, what things you would want to do. Most people, with the idea of imminent death to play with, find that there are many avenues of joy and interest that they would love to pursue. Along with that I ask them to suppose that unless they can come up with at least five redeeming qualities about themselves, they are going to be beheaded the next day. In most cases people come up with far more than five positive qualities about themselves, proving that they know in their hearts that they are worthy and deserving, even if they seem to have forgotten so in their heads. I then tell them to start focusing and suggesting to themselves that they are in fact all those wonderful things, and that life does contain many interesting things to see and do.

Sometimes people become so focused on what they think is missing from their lives that they forget to notice all the wonderful aspects that do exist. Often people become so fixated on what they think is not satisfactory about themselves, that they completely overlook all their terrific qualities. Such states of mind drain all the joy out of life and rob them of energy and vitality.

If you want your life experience to be satisfying, full of joy and wonder, then it is up to you to allow it to be, by endeavoring to see life in the best possible light. My husband says that you have to believe the best until proven wrong, and most often you will be proven correct. Assume the best of yourself and of others, and see what you come up with. Be willing to accept the life that flows through you now, and by doing so you will allow it to flow, unimpeded, into larger and more joyous realms of existence.

- 21 -

Sticking Your Neck Out

How easy it is at times just to not get involved. We certainly escape the risk of having someone angry at us, or having them think we're nuts. In my life I have seen myself swing from one to the other and, as a result, have come up with some ideas that I would like to share with you.

I first became involved with healing when I was married to Steve and living as a rancher. Because my healing experience was so overwhelming and thrilling, I constantly talked about it. I spoke of my amazing recovery and what it suggested about the nature of physical reality. I knew at times that people were bored with me, and that some even thought I was dizzy, but I couldn't keep my mouth shut. I was always amazed that people didn't want to know more, and often felt lonely and alone in my thoughts. As time went on I was called fanatical and obsessed, and I guess I was.

When my marriage to Steve ended and I moved to New York, I remained as obsessed with healing as ever. After Jerry got to know me well enough, he expressed his feelings that I was obsessed with the subject. He also objected to my emphatically negative attitude toward medical doctors, explaining that no matter how hard I wanted to believe otherwise, I was responsible for my ileostomy, not the doctors. "They only saved your life you know," he would remind me, "and there is a lot of good that they can do. They are not the demons you think they are."

"But why," I'd argue, "didn't they know anything about

healing? How could they just give me drugs and let me get worse?"

"Because," he said "that's what they know, and what they believe in, but they're not bad, and you hate them because you blame them for the illness that you created! If you think that avoiding them completely or telling others to do so is so clever, then I think you're very foolish!"

And we would go on and on like this for days, sometimes dropping it for a while, only to resume where we left off at some later date. To make matters worse, whenever Jerry had a physical complaint he would rush off to his doctor for some medication. I would get angrier and we would resume our usual argument. To me, going to a doctor seemed an admission of failure, and I was not yet ready to admit any limitations to my viewpoint. So great was my fanaticism, which was powered by my fear, that Jerry and I flew to Las Vegas to take our wedding vows because no blood test was required in Nevada. As time went on the subject became a sore spot between Jerry and me.

My teaching career allowed me to talk about healing freely. My students were very receptive, and I began to save my ideas for them alone. There were times, however, when a student came to class who was severely ill, and I found myself reluctant to lay my antidoctor rap on her. Jerry's words would resound in my head, and I'd feel the great responsibility I was taking upon my own shoulders. How terrible I thought I would feel if I prevented someone from receiving medical help, or surgical healing. I began to temper my remarks, as I realized that people seemed to take them to heart.

As time went on, Jerry's opinions began to seem wiser to me. My pleasure in life had expanded enormously, and with that my sadness and feeling of incompletion about my body had diminished. I no longer needed to hate my doctors, who I now realized were imperfect but not evil. What had happened to me wasn't their fault. While I still believed that healing concepts were necessary to gain control over illness, I could accept doctors for what they were, and not feel afraid, or that I was somehow forsaking my ideals, if I took their advice. It's fortunate for me that I came to this understanding because without it I could never have undergone reconnective surgery or taken the medication that allowed the reconnection to work.

My acceptance left me humbled, and somewhat silenced. I decided that those who sought my advice on health would have the benefit of whatever knowledge I had acquired. I would no longer, however, initiate the subject of healing every time I met a sick person. I decided not to proselytize. I was tired of trying to explain healing to people who, half of the time, felt that I was accusing them of making themselves ill, or accused me of being deluded. I felt that those who needed me would find me.

Soon, though, an event made me rethink this. I had a distant cousin who was about my age. I did not know her very well, but on the few occasions that we were together she seemed like a nice person. About five years ago I heard that she had colon cancer and was having surgery. I felt very bad, and I wondered if I should talk to her, but I feared that she and her family would think I was intruding. As her condition worsened, Sue submitted to all the medical treatment her doctors prescribed. I knew the pain that Sue and her parents were suffering, yet I still felt reluctant to interfere. "I probably won't do any good at all," I reasoned, "but I'll have them all thinking that I am accusing Sue of wanting to be ill and making light of her situation."

Sue died. She never got mad at me, neither did her parents. I never gave her the chance. I am sorry about this now. I may or may not have helped Sue, but at least I could have tried. If she felt insulted and became angry at me, I wouldn't have died. But she did. I now feel that it is worth it to stick your neck out a little, if for nothing more than knowing you've tried. When you think about it, I'm sticking my neck out now by writing this book. Of course I don't have to see any of you face-to-face and experience your reactions, but I'm still leaving myself open to all of your judgments by sharing with you my experience and my ideas. I figure you're worth it.

I want to say to all of you not to be afraid to stick your necks out. I know that it can be risky and uncomfortable, but it doesn't mean that slipping out the back door is the answer. You don't have to convert anyone to your way of thinking, but you can at least expose them to it. That's what

I'm trying to do in this book. I am not trying to force you to believe anything regarding my healing, but I am trying to encourage you to start thinking about it. Sometimes that's enough to start the ball rolling in the right direction. I wonder what would have happened if my father's friend Keith hadn't told me about Harry Edwards. Would I have recovered? Would I have created some other source of healing? I don't know. Possibly. But the fact is that knowing made a big difference. And what did Keith risk by telling me? Nothing!

I encourage all of you, as I encourage myself, to stick your necks out. Although we stand the chance of receiving ridicule and criticism, it won't harm us to say what we feel, and let the pieces fall where they will. You never know. Years later someone may begin to benefit from the information you provided.

- 22 -

My Life Now—Resolutions

As I look at my life now, the best term that I can find to describe it would be *multifaceted*. I am involved as a wife and a mother, a daughter, a sister, and a friend, a teacher, an eternal student, a writer, a singer, and a dancer. Some days I accomplish more work on my book, while other days find me completely enmeshed in family life. Sometimes I wonder how I've managed to near completion on this book, when its contents have been written in the midst of buying new school shoes, arranging play dates, birthday parties, haircuts, doctors' appointments—the list goes on and on.

One night a week I go to the Little Red School House where I sing in the parent–staff chorus. This provides joyous recreation for me. A good deal of my time and Jerry's is spent purely in the pursuit of pleasure. Finding time to be alone together, taking our boys out on our boat, or just sitting around watching videos are but a few of the ways we amuse ourselves. Having fun is important. Relaxation is valuable. We make time for both.

The desire to help others has always been present in me. I feel honored that through my teaching and now my book, I have been given the opportunity to help other human beings. My family comes first always, while friendship is extremely high on my list of priorities.

I feel fortunate to have a life so rich and full of variety. Whichever event I am involved in, I keep in mind that all the aspects are a part of the whole, and add balance to my life. As for my spiritual pursuits, I am involved in the continual learning and internalizing of ideas. I recognize that the many joys of my life were not attained by accident or by luck. I created them, through my willingness to focus and believe the best beliefs that I can. This process is never ending. I can always grow in self-love and trust. I can always use a good reminder that experience is formed from the inside out, and that I need not be afraid. Although many of these concepts have been accepted by my intellect, emotionally I have not fully recognized them. I still pace the floor all too easily if the children are out later than I had expected with their baby-sitter. My goal is to make this knowledge real not only to my mind, but to the very core of my soul. To this end I devote time every day, as you all know. I feel that in order to live life as freely and joyously as possible, I need to keep addressing these deeply important issues. Lack of trust for yourself sends you into mind trips that are aggravating and wasteful. Lack of trust for your universe creates enormous fear of danger and of your fellowman. As important as I think it is to accomplish great works in the material world, I think it is even more important to create works of beauty within your interior world. In my mind, this makes the critical difference between just getting through the events of your life and living them to the fullest.

As for myself, I use meditation as a means to look inside myself and deal with all of my ideas. Every day I need to see that those ideas are just that—ideas—and not necessarily a true picture of reality at all. If I don't, I can easily become drawn into negative beliefs, eventually ruining my day. And really, what else is there but the moment and our perception of it?

I now believe that the most important way to make my life work is to take the time to work with my beliefs. This can be done in a myriad of ways and I am not limiting this to the exercise I call Working with Beliefs. Sometimes all that is needed is time to sense yourself aside from your thoughts. I know this may sound like a difficult task, since we often perceive ourselves as our thoughts. By focusing on the sound of your breath, however, you can glimpse the presence of yourself that exists beyond your multitudinous thoughts. You may not feel anything profound, but truly it is profound to realize that you exist beyond your constant thought processes. Such detachment can help you separate yourself from some of your beliefs long enough to lessen their hold on you.

Because many of our beliefs may have been with us for centuries, changing them may not always come easy. Thus the life and death of my dear friend and teacher Jane Roberts is a case in point. No one understood more sharply and clearly the nature of beliefs and their ramifications in her life than Jane herself. Why she didn't heal herself is not an uncommon question among my students.

Jane devoted her life to bringing vital information to others. Those who knew her and studied her works know that she more than adequately accomplished her goal. It could be that she felt that her work was completed and her spirit was ready to move on. Jane and Seth always taught that a large part of our job on earth was to experience the result of our beliefs. Jane certainly experienced the results of her beliefs—beliefs that for whatever reasons she was unable or unwilling to change. She taught us all that intellectual understanding does not do the whole trick. You must live all the beliefs that you need to nurture your living. You must somehow get into your heart and mind and nervous system that you love yourself, that your being is good, and that your existence in the world is blessed. Jane understood this. She stood like a warrior and shouted it so that all of us could hear and know our worth. Where the gap was between her intellectual and emotional knowledge, I cannot say. She once told me that she wished that she had gotten into this stuff when she was as young as us kids, as she so fondly referred to us. Somewhere deep inside, Jane's fears fought hard to maintain their position, while she generously gave of her time and energy to ensure that others would stand up to theirs.

I intend to keep addressing the issue of beliefs until one day what remains are only the very best beliefs that I have to offer. I will try to do everything within my power to change my harmful and limiting ideas so that I can create the most expansive and joyous realities possible. I see this as the best way to pay tribute to the life of Jane Roberts, as well as pay tribute to my own life. I invite all of you to do the same.

Make of this what you will. It's as magical as Cinderella, as subtle and commonplace as good old common sense thinking. I do believe that we each possess a "fairy god-mother," so to speak. Call it energy, call it God, call it the power of your beliefs. As you think, so will you create; as you believe, so will you build your world.

The choice is yours. The power that can be harnessed is enormous. On the other hand, you can ignorantly allow the same power to destroy you. I certainly did. It is up to you to look inside and discover the seeds of your experience that you have planted. Are they worth watering?

Sometimes I think that a book like this might have helped me change the course of events when I first became ill. I might have sought psychiatric help, or at least changed some of my activities. If so, my life would have gone in very different directions and I would not be writing this book now. I then realize how deeply I want this book to help you, serving as a bridge into the world of psychic exploration. I know that some of my readers might, at least at first, find the idea of healing and mediumship too occult. Maybe they've had bad experiences with dishonest fortune-tellers, or grew up in a strict religious home in which these ideas were considered dangerous or even evil. I ask you, however, to consider my experience. Do you really sense anything dishonest or evil about what took place? If you do, wouldn't it be more productive for you to examine your beliefs and see what you come up with before drawing any conclusions? It would prove to be very interesting and beneficial, as your beliefs impinge on other areas of your life as well.

You will find that when you free yourself up in one area of your life, things begin to open up in others, as everything that happens to you is connected. Give yourself a break and start concentrating on some of your dreams. Discover and deal with the beliefs that stand in your way. Use the power at your disposal to create the most satisfying life that you can imagine, and then help to spread it outward to the world that you touch.

We must truly heal from the inside out—as individuals, as a species, and as a planet. We must all individually discover who we are in order to gain some understanding of the world's problems. They stem from us. We are the world.

We create it. We must all begin to know ourselves and straighten out our own misconceptions.

In one way or another most of us have been taught to be mistrustful. When I grew up, we were given two basic explanations for the origin of our species. In one we were taught that God created the earth and that he did an absolutely perfect job. Everything was going beautifully in the Garden of Eden until man, by disobeying God's orders, destroyed the perfection all around him. From this theory, it was easy to see that God was perfect, the earth was perfect, but man was a beast, and should not be trusted.

The other theory presents an accidental universe in which atoms and molecules came together for no reason at all and just happened to form into man. Of course evolution gets involved here, with survival being based on nothing more than that which is most fit. Here the notion of a soul or consciousness is completely wiped out. Nothing exists beyond the physical. Nothing is there to lend meaning or cohesiveness to physical life.

I don't know which of these two theories I dislike the most. The first admits to a God, and a divine plan, but we come out the losers in the story. We are labeled evil, and have to carry that stigma throughout our lives. The second theory gives you nothing to hold on to. You happened for no apparent reason. Your life has very little meaning and you can disappear just as easily as you appeared. I don't see how any of us could be anything but ill at ease with such ideas. How many of us unknowingly carry around guilts and fears about ourselves that we haven't even begun to examine, guilts and fears that stem from these faulty concepts as well as others?

What it comes down to is that it doesn't really matter where these faulty ideas originated. It does matter, however, that we challenge them as our main criteria for reality. Some people may not even have thought or considered how these theories may have affected them, but I bet there isn't one person reading this book who can't relate to the experience of guilt or fear. Whether our beliefs were accumulated through many lifetimes, or were formulated fresh from the time of our birth, what matters is challenging and changing those beliefs that are producing undesirable effects. By seizing the power that is ours, we can use our minds as instruments that work for us!

I feel that if human life is to continue, it will demand that more and more people alter their consciousness and begin to see that all events are formed from the inside out. If the vast majority of the population remains devoted to what Seth refers to as "the official line of consciousness,"—the picture of reality constructed by our newspapers and televisions—then people will always be doomed to fear and mistrust. I feel enormous fear about the world after listening to the evening news. I have to remind myself that despite what I hear and read, I live in a safe universe. Even if it is not safe for others, even if many are creating physical or mental disasters for themselves, I have the power to create a safe experience.

On the one hand, my life is spent running my household, loving and tending to my family and friends, teaching, writing, singing, and dancing. On the other hand, I am involved in a spiritual quest to structure my interior world with the most positive beliefs possible. I try to construct a view of reality that supports what I want and not necessarily what appears logical. If I believe in pink elephants, only to discover one day that I have been completely deluded, at least I will have relieved some of the pressure that results from living in the official line of consciousness. As Seth said in class in July of 1975, "The official line of consciousness forms a world about it, and you perceive and experience that world, and it will always show you the results of the beliefs that are inherent in the official line of consciousness. While you devote yourself to that official line of consciousness, the world will always appear the same—evil, disastrous, bound for damnation, whether through nuclear destruction, or the greater judgment of a fundamental God."

I have never thought of myself as a political person, and I still don't. I took part in two peace rallies during the Vietnam War. After I was chased by policemen carrying bats and tear gas, my revolutionary days came quickly to a halt. I used to feel guilty that I didn't work harder for causes, believing as some do that if you aren't part of the solution you are part of the problem.

I now feel that this is not the case. One doesn't have to be politically active in order to do something for the world. I've come to feel that the only real revolution is a revolution of thought, a revolution in which people truly begin to think and believe differently and therefore change their actions and projections accordingly. This type of revolution starts with the individual and works outward into the masses. It starts with people like you and me taking the time to alter our awareness so that we can become cognizant of ourselves as something more than our thoughts and opinions. We must question whether our thoughts and opinions are productive for us or not. From this perspective, we can stop believing and submitting to ideas that are bringing us undesirable results. If we can't begin to understand on an individual level how we may be making ourselves ill, or unhappy, or poverty stricken, then I don't know how we will ever truly tackle the world problems we face today. We can let the governments battle it out, which is what we have been doing, and hope for the best, but if our world goes up in flames, we will only have ourselves to blame. Again, I'm not demanding that any of you go out and demonstrate against nuclear weapons, but I am asking that you begin to examine your own perspective on human life, your own personal beliefs about yourself and your universe. Do you have prejudices and hatreds that you project outward into the universe? Do you carry around fears and guilts that you unknowingly project into the atmosphere all around you? I ask you to examine these issues because I think they are vitally connected to the reality we experience, and help form, and are responsible for.

White Eagle (a spirit communicator mentioned earlier in the text) writes, "When man truly comes to understand the importance of his thoughts, he will be more careful as to what he thinks and concentrates upon." Wailing and complaining that humankind is doomed and coming to an end only helps to ensure such doom. It is our responsibility to do this work, not just for personal benefit, but for the rest of the planet. Keep in mind that it is not only what we do in our lives that composes our challenge, either, but how we go about doing it, thinking it, creating it, and reacting to it. You can work for causes with a view so negative and powered by fear, that with all of your hard work you actually achieve more harm than good for your world. How absurd, when underneath all you really wanted to do was help. Again, you cannot truly help others until you help yourself. Then there is so much that you can do, even in just the way that you smile at someone. However, to truly give outward to your world, you have to first give inwardly to yourself, your own affirmation of yourself. That is the most that it takes. Once you can see that there is nothing wrong with you and that you can accept and love yourself, just as you are, then the heavens will open! You will have lifted the shades on the biggest windows in the world, the windows of your heart, and you will be able to experience greater love and joy than you have known before. In this way your life and your experience of it will be a blessing to the world and will benefit it whether you are aware of its ramifications or not.

I would like to conclude by saying that I see my life as being lived on many different levels, all of which form the picture you see. You all do the same thing, although some of you may be aware of the process more than others. I am concerned with my own personal life, and I am also concerned with the life of others and of my planet. I am sure that many of you feel similarly. Let us conclude that we will endeavor to make our lives about more than just getting by, or accomplishing things on the material level, as we seek to add an understanding of who we are, and what we think, to the overall picture. I think then that we can really do something to alter our existence for the better. By so doing, we ourselves become a more beautiful piece in the mosaic of life. In turn, the mosaic grows more beautiful. Beyond that, with more of us finding inner peace as we learn to accept and love ourselves, we help to maintain the serenity and balance of the planet. By honoring ourselves, we are able to honor all life. Let us start with our own lives, as we endeavor to work, play, grow, and heal, from the inside out.

Appendices
Introduction

Each of these appendices covers an alternate method of healing or spiritual development. Each is valuable, and I have tried and tested all of them. None of them, however, is a substitute for dealing with your personal beliefs.

Some of the methods will appeal to you more than others. Feel free to explore the topics that appeal to you and bypass those that don't.

I do not believe in any one cure-all. However, we each possess the power to create change in our lives. The following methods may prove useful to you in doing so. If you begin to believe in the methods, they can spur you on even further.

First, you must make the choice to create change in your life. Then you can choose a method, or a few methods to work with. If the method proves successful, it will naturally reinforce your belief in your own power. As your faith in yourself grows, so does your ability to create change in almost any situation.

Combined with working with the power of your beliefs, any of the following methods can help you obtain and maintain physical and emotional health. I offer them to you because I have found them useful. I want to state clearly, however, that I am not suggesting that you divert from whatever medical course you are on in order to explore these methods.

Appendix A
Acupuncture

Acupuncture has long been used to heal as well as to relieve pain. Originating in China as early as 1200 B.C., it is performed by inserting fine needles into specific places on the body. It has proven useful in treating many physical and emotional conditions.

My exposure to acupuncture came as a result of my relationship to Carolyn Bengston, my massage therapist; Carolyn is also a Certified Acupuncture practitioner. At our sessions, she was always kind enough to tell me of her studies, and of the wonderful healings that she witnessed as a student of acupuncture.

I've always felt that Carolyn must have lived at least one incarnation in the East because she is so completely comfortable with Chinese medicine. She has a wealth of knowledge about the human body's strengths and weaknesses, the total connection between the mind, soul, and body systems, and Chinese medicine and herbology.

After my long illness, I never expected myself to submit to acupuncture treatments willingly. The very idea of needles made me cringe. However, when Carolyn first suggested acupuncture, her gentle reassuring manner relieved my fears. Although I was not ill, I was under stress. Carolyn explained that our work together was a matter of preventative medicine. I didn't have to be suffering to benefit from acupuncture.

First she read my pulses. This was something she had done before and I was always relieved to hear that my pulses read strong and consistent. This process was not just a matter of taking my pulse. By pressing my wrist at varying depths, Carolyn could determine the pulse energies of the different organs in my body. Carolyn uses this process to confirm her intuitions about my state of health. After this she began the actual acupuncture.

I was amazed at Carolyn's light touch. I did not even feel the needles going into my body. She knew just where to place them, and within a few minutes she had finished. "Just relax now," she said, and I soon began to feel the tensions in my body ease. There was a stiffness in my back that began to loosen up as well. I almost fell asleep by the time Carolyn removed the needles twenty minutes later. As always, I left her home feeling relaxed.

Carolyn used acupuncture to relieve a cold—"jump starting my liver," she refers to it—and to induce relaxation. Although my liver is well, my earlier, serious liver disease and the medication I take for regulating digestion suggested the need for such treatments as a preventative.

I have grown to rely on my treatments with Carolyn. I feel better knowing that someone is consistently checking my pulses and discussing the state of my body and emotions with me. Because she has much more knowledge to impart regarding her work, I am honored that Carolyn granted me the following interview.

Sheri: When did you first become involved in acupuncture and why?

Carolyn: Interestingly enough, it came as an evolvement of Swedish massage, and my massage treatments over the past few years. I wanted to expand my knowledge of the energy that travels through the body: what it is, where it gets blocked, and how to get it moving more efficiently. I wanted to develop a deeper involvement of moving the energy of the body. When I was in college, Chinese art history was my minor. I've always had a fascination for China and Chinese thought and philosophy. I grew up in San Francisco. My grandmother had gone to Chinese practitioners there. This goes back to the late 1940s and early Fifties. I remember her having tremendous relief with her bursitis, so it's been on my mind and in my being for a long time. It really evolved, however, out of massage and my experience with that. I attended many workshops. One thing that was a great influence is something called Jin Shin Jyutsu. That is really the beginning of acupuncture with the hands. It's the hands form of acupuncture. I was impressed by how dynamic it was. The hands of the practitioner released various areas of the client just by touch in certain patterns. This process made me even more curious as to how dynamic the needles would be. So it really came out of that.

Sheri: How long have you studied acupuncture?

Carolyn: My school has a three-year program. It's the Tri State Institute for Traditional Chinese Acupuncture, and the director has had a tremendous influence on my career as an acupuncturist. I've had many teachers. There is a lovely Japanese woman who also has had a tremendous influence on me. She has developed her own style, which is very Japanese-oriented. She's extremely into the body, feeling the body, touching the body. She feels where energy is stuck with her hands. Then through various patterns she has studied for years, certain points are put together to release those blocked areas. That's a powerful influence and is something that I will be very involved with in my own practice.

Sheri: Can you explain the principle through which acupuncture works?

Carolyn: If you believe that the energy of the body is continuous, and if you believe that disease or illness is stuck energy, what these patterns of points will do is release that stuckness and allow it to move or help it move a little quicker. Think of electricity and the switches on an electrical line. If you turn the switch on, the radio goes on. If you turn the switch off, the radio goes off. It's sort of like that. The needle is almost turning on a switch or opening up a circuit.

Sheri: So in essence, acupuncture is used to move energy through the body, stuck energy, to circulate the energy and reroute it. Now, the different acupuncture points, I know there are way too many of them for you to go into each of them. Could you, however, talk a little about the acupuncture points?

Carolyn: You have to go back to the various organ functions of the body. The spleen will do something like make blood; it also promotes the digestive tract. If a person is having tremendous digestive problems, then you would use points in the spleen meridian because that meridian is in charge of digestion and making blood. Now, the liver is in charge of the smooth flow of things, of all things. It's in charge of keeping things going and circulating. Therefore, if someone is having a lot of menstrual cramps, we would more than likely go to the liver meridian and, by palpation even, find points that are very sore. We would then use those points along the liver meridian to ease menstrual cramps. We think of the kidney as the root of life. If someone has lower back pain in the kidney area, or other keepings that go along with the kidney, such a lot of fatigue or asthma that's been around for many years, so that the kidney is not able to go up and grasp energy from the lung and bring it back down into the body properly, we might use some kidney points. As you see, it becomes very involved. That's why it takes at least three years of study to begin to grasp.

Sheri: Can you tell me of some cases that you have witnessed or worked with in which you've seen acupuncture bring about positive changes?

Carolyn: I've seen a lot. I've seen people with tremendous migraine headaches recover completely in as little as five or six treatments. And that is done by finding out what kind of headache you are dealing with. It could be digestive. On the other hand, if it's just stuck energy in the back of the head that's not allowed to go through, you can open up the back of the head, so to speak. If it's a deficient liver we can go through the liver meridian and the gall bladder meridian, which is connected along the sides of the head, and open that up and release the energy because again, pain and illness is stuck energy. So a migraine headache is great to work with because usually it's energy that's stuck in the back and is just not going up to the head. In fact, anything that happens in the face—cataracts, poor eyesight, sinusitis, ringing in the ears—much of the time is just a matter of the energy being stuck across the top of the shoulders, not flowing in or out of the head.

Sheri: I get the sense then that absolutely everything is connected to everything else.

Carolyn: Everything is connected to everything else.

Sheri: Therefore, if one thing isn't working, it's very likely that its connection to something else is blocked.

Carolyn: And it's going to manifest itself somewhere ultimately, and how that particular individual manifests is a clue as to what meridian.

Sheri: By meridian you mean the acupuncture point?

Carolyn: Yes, and what patterns to put together.

Sheri: The patterns would be formed by using a combination of meridians?

Carolyn: Yes. The best thing to do ultimately is to find the cause of the manifestation. Signs and symptoms are really just a clue to give us information as to what's causing where the weakness is, where the energy is blocked, where it's getting hot. Really, ultimately you have to find the cause.

Sheri: Now, let's say that you determine that the cause is also emotional, which in so many cases it is, then you can use acupuncture to work with the emotions?

Carolyn: Smooth flow of emotions, absolutely. There are basically five emotions that we work from. Fear has to do with the root of life. We relate that most times to kidney and bladder, which in terms of elements is a water problem. It relates to something happening with the water in the body. There's anger, which is wood, and it's controlled and part of the liver and gall bladder meridian. There's joy or lack of joy, which is the heart, heart fire. There's people that have what I would describe as a movie in their mind. It's as if their minds just don't stop thinking. They are having conversations all of the time and they're overly sympathetic to things. That's part of the spleen or earth. They're usually over nourishing, or they have not gotten enough nourishment from life for themselves. The last emotion would be grief, which is ruled by the lung function. So the emotions are all tied in again with all the elements and all the organs. Most things are emotional. When there is an emotional problem, we first take a look at the liver because it's in charge of the smooth flow of all things. Then we take a deeper look into the individual emotion and unblock the corresponding meridian. Through this means we can move the energy—allowing change to take place.

Sheri: Do you recommend acupuncture to people as preventative medicine?

Carolyn: If a person enjoys body work and is a believer in preventative medicine, I think acupuncture is a fine way to do that.

Sheri: For people with any kind of problem do you feel that acupuncture has the possibility of promoting healing?

Carolyn: Yes, it does. Acupuncture is not a cure. What it does do is release blocked energy. In this day and age it is almost impossible to maintain a balance in the body, and acupuncture in its simplest form is just a pure balancing of the energies, so it is good for everyone in that sense. It goes beyond that, however. It is an energetic field that can be smoothed out.

Sheri: Would you say that you've seen a number of types of illnesses respond to this form of treatment?

Carolyn: Yes.

Sheri: What about chronic illnesses?

Carolyn: Now, chronicity takes a long time, because usually people take a long time to develop it.

Sheri: Have you seen work with AIDS patients?

Carolyn: Yes, people are doing it. There are clinics with AIDS and acupuncture now just to tone the immune system. I've seen AIDS patients who are living fuller lives; their symptoms seem to decrease a little bit, and their life is prolonged. Emotionally they are helped. They seem to relax more easily, and their fear is alleviated some. There are all sorts of things that AIDS and acupuncture are doing.

Sheri: It seems as though acupuncture is something that we ought to expose more people to in this country.

Carolyn: It is happening. In California acupuncture is all over the place. The East Coast is a little more conservative, but it is growing.

Sheri: What about between the coasts?

Carolyn: There is a lot going on in New Mexico, Utah, Detroit, Florida—actually, it is all over. The main thing to think about concerning acupuncture is that it really is an energetic process. We don't really work on specific diseases. We work on releasing stuck energy and getting the energy to flow smoothly in a balanced manner.

Sheri: In which case a disease could be weakened or alleviated or overcome.

Carolyn: Exactly.

Sheri: So in essence, you work on the whole being. By strengthening the being their weaknesses become weaker, their strengths become stronger.

Carolyn: Yes.

I am very grateful to Carolyn for sharing this information with us. I'm sure that many of you can see the inherent value in acupuncture. Again, as with all the methods recommended in this book, I stress that you do not place the power in the methodology alone, but always endeavor to recognize your own vastly important role in healing yourself. Although help is available, and I truly recommend availing yourself of any and every useful tool at your disposal, it is you who creates your health or lack of it. Healers such as Carolyn can work to put us back together, but they cannot prevent us from taking ourselves apart.

Therefore, while seeking help from others, always try to understand the causes behind your difficulties. Work internally to change and balance your ways of thinking. The keys to the harmony that will ensure your health are within you now. As Carolyn said, "Acupuncture is not a cure. What it does do is release blocked energy. In its simplest form acupuncture is just a pure balancing of the energies." You can learn to understand why your energy has become blocked, and directly address the issues and beliefs involved. By doing so, you can begin your own energy balancing process, thus aiding the practitioner, rather than working against his or her efforts. In the ideal situation the patient and the practitioner work together. In this way you can make sure that the results you achieve are not short-lived.

I have written of my own experience with acupuncture to illustrate that it is not frightening, dangerous, or painful. It is a system of healing that could prove very beneficial to you. You may, therefore, want to explore it more thoroughly. I recommend reading a book entitled *Plain Talk about Acupuncture*. (For further information, see references.)

Appendix B
Homeopathic Medicine

I first became interested in homeopathic medicine when I wanted to replace the medication I take to regulate my bowel with something gentler. Although I was unable to make a change (deficiencies are probably the most difficult problems to treat homeopathically), I did learn quite a bit about homeopathic medicine. I have been very impressed with the effectiveness of these gentle remedies, which I use freely now on myself, my husband, and my children.

In 1984 I was fortunate to meet Luke Gatto, a teacher of homeopathic medicine, who introduced me to its use in the home. According to Luke, "Homeopathy is a science and an art. Homeopathy means matching like remedies with like pathology. When you take a homeopathic remedy, it is matching the symptoms or the vibrational quality of a disease, which clears it. Matching energies with like energies neutralizes those energies and throws off disease."

Homeopathy was founded in the early 1800s by a German physician by the name of Samuel Hahnemann. At the time people were being treated for malaria with quinine (cinchona bark) water. Although a very powerful treatment, it was accompanied by strong side effects. Dr. Hahnemann wondered what the effect would be if a healthy person took quinine. He therefore began an experiment of taking quinine and discovered that it could cause in a *healthy* person symptoms similar to those of the disease it cured in a *sick* person. He then decided to try diluting the quinine. He eventually diluted it down to one part of quinine to one million parts of water. He found that the new homeopathic medication referred to as cinchona or china, had profound results. He discovered that homeopathic china helped with symptoms of flu, as well as the exhaustion that often follows a flu. It is considered valuable as a basic health tonic. This was how homeopathy was born.

There are now many homeopathic remedies. Many people are baffled by the infinitesimal amounts of the original substance that are diluted in such medicines. Many people are convinced they work. Derived from plant, animal, and mineral substances, these remedies possess properties that stimulate the body's curative response to disease. According to Luke, there are remedies for every ailment known to man, when deduced properly.

What I find reassuring about the use of homeopathy is precisely *potencies*, the dilutedness of its remedies. I have given them to my children for coughs, colds, fever, teething, growing pains, and stomachaches. Never have they experienced an unpleasant side effect, and yet I am certain that they have been relieved of discomfort. Because so many remedies can be used for the same symptom, much trial and error is required. If the remedy is not the correct one, it is believed that nothing will happen. If it is correct, an improvement may be experienced almost immediately.

Indeed, you learn about homeopathy through its use. After a while you become familiar with the remedies that serve you and your family and feel very at ease using them. You can purchase a homeopathic first-aid kit as well as a book on the subject. In the kit you will find a number of useful remedies accompanied with a list of how to use them. A good book will provide explanations of the remedies for specific symptoms. This is where you become the expert. You choose a remedy based not only on the symptom you are dealing with, but on the nature and personality of the person who has the symptom. Many factors are taken into consideration. It helps to make a note of all the remedies you try and their results. In no time you will feel comfortable about using these gentle substances.

Luke had warned me that prescription or over-the-counter medications easily render the gentle homeopathic medicines useless. While I'm sure he's right, I use homeopathic remedies even though I take medication regularly. I find that the remedies still work for me.

Again, remember to use your common sense when exploring any new field of healing. If you have a serious illness, it is not advisable to disregard your physician's advice. In my opinion you can explore homeopathy without fear. On the other hand, if my child has an illness that concerns me, I take him to see his pediatrician.

I purchase literature and remedies from two homeopathic pharmacies in Pennsylvania. Boiron-Borneman, Inc. is located in Norwood. Boericke & Tafel is located in Philadelphia. Both carry a wide variety of books and remedies of the highest quality. (For more information see references.)

I have recently purchased remedies for flu, coughs, and sore throats. They are made up of four or more remedies combined together. I have already found these to be useful with my children and they eliminate some of the guesswork out of which remedy to use. Luke often combines remedies from the first-aid kit. To begin with, however, you may feel reluctant. If this is the case, take your time and experience one remedy at a time.

The following material was written by Luke about his experience with homeopathy:

"I was given two years to live by my medical doctors. They had consulted with me about a kidney disease I had inherited from my mother, who was at that time ill and dependent on dialysis. The doctor insisted I go on dialysis as well. I refused. Instead, I turned to homeopathic medicine. My first experience with a homeopathic remedy was one chosen specifically for aluminum poisoning, called Alumina 30X; 30X was the potency I needed at the time. I took this prescribed homeopathic treatment for aluminum toxicity over a two-week period and my kidney condition improved so dramatically that I felt like a renewed and vigorous young man again. My blood tests improved so incredibly that the doctors were stunned. Even my so-called irreversibly scarred kidney became *unscarred* over a two-year period of treatment with good nutrition and homeopathy! The scarring actually dissolved and reversed to normal healthy tissue.

"I never again have used allopathic medicine (synthetic drugs) for any health problem since. I studied and learned all that I could about homeopathic medicine, natural whole foods for sound nutrition, and herbal remedies. Ten years have passed and I am healthy and intend to stay that way by continuing to employ homeopathic medicine for any health problem that arises.

"Homeopathic remedies are inexpensive, easy to use and take, and fascinating to learn about. You do not need to have a medical background to use and apply a first-aid kit for yourself and your family. It is advisable to consult with a good homeopathic practitioner in your local area for chronic problems, however.

"Over the years I have found that homeopathy has proven to be a strong and consistent solution for many forms of illness and disease, without having to suppress symptoms or cause harmful side effects. I sincerely hope that more and more health authorities will open themselves up to experiencing homeopathy in the future. The public deserves to hear about these alternative therapies!"

Luke Gatto is a research biologist and cofounder of the Ojai Foundation in Ojai, California. He travels widely, lecturing on homeopathy and nutrition. (For more information see references.)

Appendix C
Diet and Fitness

While I do not intend to get into a long discussion about foods, I want to remind you that a sound diet will do a lot to ensure your health. Dr. Max Warmbrand was the first person to expose me to the idea of sound nutrition. I met him during my bout with chronic hepatitis. He was the first medical person who felt I could overcome the affliction in my body. He had been treating people with foods for his entire career and had witnessed all types of illness overcome through simple sound nutrition. When I examine the Warmbrand diet, I see one simple principle emerge: "Eat as the serfs did! Eat wholesome foods that grow in the earth. Do not overcook food. Do not overseason."

Carol A. Nostrand is a friend and a diet consultant. Her cookbook, *A Handbook for Improving Your Diet* (see references), helps you to make simple changes in your eating habits. If you are uninformed about foods, and especially if your health is suffering, take the opportunity to educate yourself in this area. If you are well, improving your diet can help you stay that way.

Again, your health is your responsibility. If it is failing you, there is a lot that can be achieved through simple sound nutrition. At one time in the past my husband was experiencing difficulty with high blood pressure. He went to see Dr. Robert Atkins, who is well known for his work with hypertension and heart disease. His suggestions involved lowering sugar, sodium, and fat intake while increasing vitamin and mineral intake. Jerry followed his dietary instructions and also began to work with meditation and aerobic exercise to reduce stress. The result was a complete recovery. Dr. Atkins's book, *Nutrition Breakthrough*, is well worth reading.

Again, one's beliefs will determine how far they want to go with this. I am not a perfectionist when it comes to foods. I try to make healthy wholesome foods for my family but I do not deny my children or myself sugar completely. Some nutritionists believe in strict macrobiotic diets. Most diet consultants are very negative about dairy products, believing that they invite allergies and are mucus producing. My first son practically lived on yogurt for the first five years of his life. Most kids are big milk drinkers. Some believe that you should eat no red meat at all but think chicken and fish are acceptable. After a while you can go a little crazy thinking of all the foods that you supposedly should not eat.

My suggestion is to use common sense and take the middle road. Try to avoid excesses, educate yourself about foods, and try to eat as many healthy wholesome foods as you can. But as Jane Roberts once said to me, "A TV dinner served with love can do more for a family than all the healthy foods in the world served under strict sterile conditions."

I believe that you are more what you think than what you eat. Then again, if you believe that you had better not eat certain foods, you ought to stay away from them. I think the solution rests in outlining a diet that works for you, one that contains life-giving properties while still providing joyous eating pleasure. Diet consultants and good books can be very helpful in achieving this.

Along with all these considerations it is wise to institute some form of exercise into your life. Practically everyone will benefit from exercise. Again you want to use common sense, picking a type of exercise that is compatible with you. Let your body adjust and grow used to a level of movement before you increase it.

It makes sense to assume that a body that exercises will be stronger than a body that doesn't. Aerobic exercise is known to build strong hearts and stamina, increasing your heart rate and thereby pumping blood throughout your body at an accelerated rate. In so doing it cleanses the arterial and venous walls of your circulatory system.

As stated over and over in this book, your health is your responsibility. Knowledge of healing works to ensure your good health, as well as the health of your family. Take the opportunity to read up on areas in which you are uninformed, and educate yourself now. What you do today may pay off huge dividends in the future!

Appendix D
Bach Flower Remedies

Bach Flower Remedies are gentle substances derived from wildflower blossoms. Dr. Edward Bach, M.B., B.S., L.R.C.P., D.P.H., created them over four years. In 1930 he began this work, leaving behind a successful medical practice in London. It was his desire to create a system of medicine that could heal the sick without producing harmful side effects.

What I love about Dr. Bach is his spiritualism. He believed that all the ills of mankind were the result of emotional conflicts. He was less interested in the physical symptoms of a patient than in the feelings and emotions that gave rise to the particular symptoms. He felt that if one was in harmony with oneself and the universe, one would virtually be immune to disease.

Many of us have been taught to mistrust. The stress of living further adds to feelings of uneasiness and insecurity. The demands on people to produce and provide often overwhelm them. They barely have time to examine their feelings, or to think about the deeper aspects of living. Their lives are spent in the pursuit of achievement with very little thought to spiritual growth. To Dr. Bach's mind, that alone could justify the vast amount of human suffering on the earth today.

Dr. Bach decided that in order to treat disease one had to first treat the emotions that gave rise to disease. He developed thirty-eight remedies derived from herbal flowers. The thirty-eight remedies are placed under the following seven headings:

1. for insufficient interest in present circumstances

2. for uncertainty

3. for fear

4. for loneliness

5. for those oversensitive to influences and ideas

6. for overcare for welfare of others

7. for despondency or despair

Dr. Bach believed that treating these emotional states promoted wholeness. Vitality would increase, and this needed strength would restore health.

Like homeopathic remedies, the Bach flower remedies are very gentle and pure. Therefore it is believed that you cannot harm yourself by taking them too often. Also it is considered harmless to take a larger-than-prescribed dosage. However, only a tiny quantity is necessary. The remedies come in liquid form in small bottles. The instructions tell you to put two drops of the remedy into a small amount of water, which you can then drink. They have very little taste and are easy to ingest. The Bach Flower Remedies have been known to produce remarkable results. Although unusual and controversial, thousands of cases seem to have demonstrated their effectiveness.

Dr. Bach did not wish to cloud the miraculous nature of these gentle remedies with theories. He believed the universe automatically provided herbs containing healing properties. He did not feel that this needed to be explained, any more than wild animals needed to explain why certain plants aided them when they were ill.

What Dr. Bach does offer is thirty-eight wonderful remedies. I have used quite a few of them at different points in my life. If I feel that I am going through an emotionally difficult time, I analyze my emotions. Along with belief work, I take a remedy for a few weeks that correlates to my particular set of feelings. No matter how cloudy my mood, eventually the sun always comes out.

Dr. Bach felt that this certainly was a good form of preventative medicine. Long before physical symptoms surface, one's mood would indicate a disturbance. By dealing with the disturbance at its onset, one could prevent the symptoms from ever arising.

Again, as in homeopathy, the best way to learn about the Bach Flower Remedies is through their use. Since they are considered completely pure and harmless you have nothing to lose. I recommend reading *The Bach Flower Remedies*, which include three books in one volume: *Heal Thyself* by Edward Bach; *The Twelve Healers* by Edward Bach; and *The Bach Flower Repertory* by Dr. F. J. Wheeler (for further information see references). This small yet valuable book describes each remedy so that you can begin working with them. It will also give you an understanding of Dr. Bach's philosophy of life and health.

Appendix E
Crystals

It's hard not to notice how popular crystals have become. People are buying them, giving them as gifts, wearing them around their necks, displaying them in their homes, and using them for many different purposes. Right now I am sitting in my study, surrounded by crystals of all shapes and sizes. While the power to create change lies within us, I believe that crystals can enhance that power.

Most naturally occurring quartz crystal (silicon dioxide) was formed 100 to 250 million years ago and has what is referred to as piezo-electric properties. This means that it can store, amplify, transmit, or alter electrical charges. Because quartz crystals maintain a consistent, even vibratory pattern, they are used to synchronize clocks and watches. Quartz crystals are also used to amplify sound in microphones and loudspeakers. In computers quartz crystals help to store large amounts of data, and in laser technology, quartz is used to focus energy in order to (for example) measure the distance to the moon or to perform delicate eye surgery.

Each quartz crystal is unique and clear, like frozen water. When other minerals are included within the quartz crystal, the quartz takes on other colors and properties. Amethyst is purple, rose quartz is pink, smoky quartz is gray and Tourmaline of many colors, all the way from black to pink. There are many beautiful and useful crystals. While clear quartz is the most versatile, each type of crystal possesses its own unique qualities.

Amethyst, for example, is considered to be very powerful for meditation. Because amethyst is known to help calm the thinking mind, it serves to open the channels of awareness to the deeper portions of ourselves. Rose quartz is known as the healer of the heart. It opens the heart channels and promotes healing of internal wounds. It encourages greater self-love, which naturally brings along with it greater inner peace and fulfillment.

For in-depth information about different crystals and their use I recommend reading *Crystal Enlightenment* (see references).

Although we have been relying on quartz for such a long time in terms of our technology, only recently are people, on a wide scale, becoming interested in the other uses. Still, many people balk at the idea of taking crystals seriously. Yet, if a slice of crystal can store memory in a computer, then why can't it hold thoughts or ideas? If crystal can synchronize accurate time in watches through its vibratory pattern, then maybe it can actually help us to synchronize and balance ourselves. Isn't it possible that we could think our best thoughts into our crystal, to be drawn upon when needed? Couldn't we program our crystals to work for us in certain ways?

Again, as in everywhere in this book, I do not say to any of you that you must believe this. I do suggest, however, that you kick it around, and see what you come up with. Purchase a crystal and experiment with it. You don't have to have any deep belief in order to try some experimentation.

If you do not already have a crystal, I recommend that you purchase one small point of quartz. Don't make your selection based on sight alone. Take the time to hold a few crystals in your hand. You may sense that one crystal is more attuned to your being. If you have a strong feeling about a certain crystal, buy it. Spend some time each day holding your crystal as you begin to grow more familiar with it, and it with you! The following exercise will help you to begin to use and get to know as well as energize your crystal.

Energizing and Using Your Crystal

Step One: Hold your crystal in one of your hands. (Some books tell you to hold it in your left hand, while other books will tell you that there are right-handed and left-handed crystals. My opinion is that you should hold your crystal with the hand that wants to hold it, and if you feel no preference, you can try one hand this time and the other hand the next.)

Step Two: Begin meditating on your breath, using the sound *sohom* to help you focus in on your breathing.

Step Three: As you inhale, see yourself drawing energy into you.

Step Four: As you exhale, envision the energy going through you into the crystal.

Step Five: Repeat Steps Three and Four a few times. That will allow you to charge yourself and your crystal with energy. Now imagine what you desire. You may desire healing to take place in your body, or for a particular situation to come about in your life. Whatever it may be, envision it as clearly as possible in your mind. You can then take your crystal and place it on your body in places where you wish for healing to take place, envisioning all the while that the energy is coming through the crystal into you.

If you work with this for a while, you will begin to observe your crystal grow warm with energy. Through continuity of thought you can program your crystal to ease pain and promote healing. You can imagine that your crystal is a flashlight and envision energy emanating from it. In your mind move the flashlight over your body from head to toe. See the white healing energy entering into you. If you have pain, place the crystal directly on that part of your body after you have already charged your crystal with energy. Imagine that the energy from your crystal is entering you and soothing the pain away. As you do this you will be continually charging your crystal with thoughts.

Include your crystal in your work with the Five-Phase Healing Program. It may increase the effectiveness of visualization and working with beliefs. I think you will find crystals useful in a myriad of ways once you begin working with them.

Appendix F
Working with Dreams

Although we spend a third of our lives dreaming, many of us remain unimpressed by our dreams. We engage in them daily, awaken sometimes with our mood drastically affected, and yet it is a rare person who goes out of his way to recall a dream or record it.

I, like most people, thought very little about my dreams until I began attending Jane Roberts's classes. At that point I couldn't help but examine my dreams more closely. Seth discussed dreams often, describing them in far grander terms than I had ever imagined. According to Seth, our dreams are not just a bunch of nonsensical cartoons, taking place for no reason at all. Instead they are real events, taking place in space as valid as the physical reality that we know. The dream state is not just an imaginary zone, but a truly valid reality in which the events taking place have meaning. These events touch our lives in many ways and are formulated in large by our beliefs.

Seth suggested that we each keep a dream notebook to record all of the dreams we were able to recall. The simple act of keeping a notebook by the side of the bed immediately impressed upon my subconscious mind that I would remember my dreams. I also began to suggest to myself, prior to falling asleep, that I would remember my dreams when I awoke in the morning.

Nothing convinced me more thoroughly of the scope and validity of dream activity than the study of my own dreams that ensued. At first my dreams read back to me like strange stories. As I began to interpret them, however, I occasionally could see how I was acting out fears and desires within them. I still reserved judgment about their validity. I kept recording those dreams that I could remember and let it go at that.

Then in May of 1976 my father had a massive heart attack. I returned home to New Jersey to be by his side as he fought for his life in the same hospital where I had fought so hard for my own. My sister and brothers joined me as we tried to send our love and energy to our father. He managed to stay alive in the hospital for five days and died on the fifth day in emergency open-heart surgery.

During the following week we dealt with the loss of our father and the countless people who filled our home to pay their respects to Herman. During this time I neglected to record any dreams. I had left my dream notebook behind on the farm.

After two weeks back at the farm I opened my dream notebook and began to browse through it. I was astonished when I came upon a dream recorded two weeks prior to my father's heart attack. I had retained no memory of this dream. If I had not written it down, I never would have known I had it. In the dream my brother Richard was a surgeon. He had to perform open-heart surgery on a male patient. Although this patient was not described as my father, my sister, brother, mother, and I were all very involved in the case, and extremely concerned about its outcome. We sat in the waiting room throughout the entire operation in tremendous fear for the life of the patient. After what seemed like an eternity we were informed that the patient had died. We were heartbroken. The last sentence of the dream reads, "We are all crying as if out of control, it's so horrible."

I was amazed. This dream was so reminiscent of the day my father had died that I felt certain it related to my father's death. I was floored to discover that the material had come out of my psyche prior to the physical event.

I now began to follow my dreams more closely, realizing that they might make very little sense to me at first but would eventually become clearer. Some of my dreams seemed incomprehensible, while others were definitely related to my life. I would dream about a conversation that would later occur. Certainly it was becoming clear to me that in my dreams I could glimpse the future, or at least the probable future, and I took part in events that were undoubtedly related to my emotions. If I was angry at someone, I might dream of yelling at them, and if I was frightened of a certain situation, I might find myself engaged in it. The more I studied my dreams, the more impressed I became with their validity and usefulness. I could gain information and perspective about situations. I could release and work out emotions. I could even help myself to make decisions based on dream information.

I began to discover that I could effect change in my dreams through suggestions. My "tidal wave" dream illustrates this. A few times every year, I dreamed I was standing on the shore or in the ocean when a huge tidal wave would form in the distance. My terror would mount as I saw the huge wall of water moving ever closer, knowing that when it crashed down on me, my life would be over. The dream would always end abruptly, just before my death. I would wake up nervous. I felt that the dream showed my fears of being vulnerable, unsafe, and out of control. I hoped the dream would change as I changed my beliefs about security. It did.

A few years after beginning my belief work, striving to see myself as safe and in control, I found myself back in my tidal-wave dream. This time I found myself in the ocean, with the wave forming behind me. Instead of accepting the scenario as usual, I said in my head, "This is my dream, and I am safe, and nothing can harm me." Before I knew what was happening, I materialized a surfboard and rode the wave exuberantly onto shore. It felt exhilarating. I am certain that it symbolized my greater security and control of my life. I don't recall ever having the tidal-wave dream again.

Another set of dreams that remains in my mind concerns the birth of my son. For years before adopting Aaron, I dreamed that I gave birth to a baby boy. In the dreams the pleasure and satisfaction were so great that I always felt deeply saddened upon awaking and discovering that in reality the baby did not exist. Sometimes I would try desperately to fall back to sleep and resume the dream, but was only able to do so once. When many years later Jerry and I decided to adopt a baby, I felt certain that the child would be a boy. Both my children have fulfilled the dream prophecy, as I have two sons.

Sometimes dreams can affect more than one person. For instance, I once dreamed I was angry at Jerry and turned to our friend Rich for consolation. The next morning Jerry reported that he had dreamed that I was upset with him and sought out Rich for comfort. Later that day Rich phoned and said that he dreamed that Jerry and I had an argument and that I had called him for advice. I think this shows that in the dream state we actually interact with other people.

It is helpful to remember that every individual who takes part in a certain dream may not recall the dream. You may have a very clear memory of a dream involving you with someone who doesn't have any memory of that dream at all. Keep in mind that another's lack of recall doesn't invalidate your dream. We each remember what is significant to us. However, what pleases me about the dream concerning myself, Jerry, and Rich is that we all did recall it. It further confirms the validity of dream experience.

Another dream that I want to describe concerns my older son, Aaron. Prior to going to sleep one evening, I was angry and frustrated with him, going through what my mother refers to as the ups and downs of raising children. I dreamed that Jerry and I had put the boys on an ocean liner and the ship had sunk. Daniel was somehow rescued, but Aaron went down with the ship. All that remained of him was a little box that he stuffed with chocolates for me, and a card that read, "I love you, Mommy."

I woke up in the middle of the night crying, only to return to the dream when I fell asleep again. When the sun rose, I awoke with my deep feelings of love for Aaron greatly renewed. I felt grateful for his life and presence in mine, and looked adoringly at him as he strode into my bedroom to say good morning. Although the day brought its usual share of disagreements over the amount of candy and television I would allow, the message in the dream was not lost. It served to remind me how blessed and beautiful the love between parent and child is.

In 1966, while still living in Ecuador, Clarence Dougherty

had dreams of Manhattan. "I dreamed that I came out to a narrow street. I saw tall women wearing miniskirts and mink coats. All around were tall buildings and black Cadillacs. I came to New York from Ecuador in 1968. I acquired my first job on Wall Street. As I walked out onto Wall Street I saw tall women wearing miniskirts and mink coats. I saw tall buildings, black Cadillacs, and the same narrow street as in the dream. I knew I had seen this very scene before."

In a dream notebook of Jerry's I discovered a very interesting dream. It was written two years before we met in Manhattan. During this time I was attending Seth classes regularly but Jerry was not. Many of his friends were there, however, and Steve and I had become friendly with his friend Rick Stack. Rick had visited the farm a couple of times. From Jerry's dream notebook: "Rick took me to a farm to meet a woman who was a dream healer. I was immediately attracted to her. She came over to me and said, 'Why didn't you notice me?' I answered that I noticed her right away. I said, 'I know who you are and I believe in you.'" When I read this dream I immediately felt that the woman Jerry dreamed about was me. Funny, too, because when I am feeling doubtful about myself it is not uncommon for me to ask Jerry if he believes in me!

I have cited these dreams to illustrate the many ways that dream activity can be useful, informative, and prophetic. There is much written about the value of dreams. I of course recommend the Seth books for further investigation. Nothing, however, can give you greater insight or understanding of your dreams than your own study of them. Incidentally, since my father's death, I have had a number of very vivid dreams in which he and I are together. It's comforting, and helps me to miss him less, for in my experience we have met again.

If you are not doing it already, pay closer attention to your dreams. You will find that they can be therapeutic as well as informative. Through working out problems in your dreams, you can help to restore your health and energy. Undoubtedly dreams can help you to understand your present experience more thoroughly. Recurring themes can tell you a good deal about your beliefs and state of mind.

As always, keep in mind that beliefs are all powerful. If

you believe that it is beyond you to remember your dreams, you will probably have difficulty remembering them. If you believe that your dreams are silly, they will appear that way. If you believe that there is a message within your dreams but you can't understand it, you will find your dreams difficult to interpret. Therefore, it may take some adjustments in your belief systems before you can fully utilize your dream state as effectively as you would like. I can only urge you keep trying. The information is there waiting for you to access it. Suggest to yourself before falling asleep that you will remember and understand your dreams upon arising. In the morning when you wake up, before you fully focus your attention outward, run through whatever dream material you can recall. If time allows you to do so, write the material down. You will be amazed to see the world of information that your dreams will make available to you.

Dreams are drastically affected by our moods. If you are going through a depressing time in your life, you will probably experience some depressing dreams. In this situation, Seth suggests that before going to sleep you suggest to yourself that you will have a pleasant, happy dream that will restore your good feelings and energy. In many cases the depression will be lightened when you awake.

The dream state is readily available to you every time that you sleep. It is not beyond any of you to make use of what already belongs to you. As I see it, any event, physical or not, that takes up at least one third of our existence ought to be worth investigating!

Appendix G
Working with the Psychic Sciences

The psychic or spiritual sciences have existed for centuries and are quite popular today. It is not uncommon for people to identify themselves by their astrological sign or to go for psychic readings.

Whether you are aware of the process or not, you create your experience in accordance with what you believe and concentrate on. As you grow in self-awareness you develop a greater understanding of how you are forming the events of your life. Your possession or lack of health, joy, or sadness becomes part of your experience that you are able to connect to the way you think and believe. Therefore, any source of information regarding our own strengths and weaknesses, tendencies and aspirations can serve as a guide to developing self-awareness.

The psychic sciences have served as guides and teaching tools for many people. Those who study astrology, numerology, and the tarot will tell you that these sciences follow quite natural universal laws and can be practical and useful tools for self-understanding.

I had my first experience with the psychic sciences when I met an actual clairvoyant. I was quite amazed by this woman's abilities. Although prior to our meeting she knew nothing about my life, within a few minutes she told me about my difficult time with illness. She went on to say that I had survived in order to help others and predicted that I would one day work in some form of healing. She predicted a second marriage for me (at the time I had just married

Steve) and concluded that my work would be helpful to many people. After I met her I realized that true clairvoyance actually exists.

I now believe we are all far more clairvoyant than we realize. Our minds contain information regarding future events as well as events affecting others. Of course, again, our beliefs determine how much of this material we will actually allow ourselves to access but it is nonetheless available to us.

Some of you may be interested in opening up your own psychic channels. You may want to develop your intuitive abilities. If this is the case, I suggest that first you accept the belief that you are indeed psychic now. Then suggest to yourself that your own connection to your inner self and intuitions will strengthen. Then observe your own thought processes. After a while you will begin to realize that many of your thoughts are intuitive and always have been. More than likely you have just been unaware of them.

Suggestions can more easily take root in your psyche when your mind is in an open, susceptible state. Therefore, if you really want to encourage psychic development, apply your suggestions while working with the Five-Phase Healing Program. As always, focus on the sound of your breath to induce relaxation through meditation. If you desire, add characterized breathing, and as you exhale suggest that you are eliminating all tension, cares, and worries from your mind. Once you have done this to a point where you feel sufficiently relaxed and clearheaded, begin to suggest that you are already psychic and that clairvoyant abilities exist within you. Along with that, suggest that as time goes on you will become more aware of the intuitive nature of your thoughts. You might want to repeat this suggestion for five or ten minutes. Then move on to other areas. It is not necessary to linger with one suggestion for any greater length of time than that, in one sitting.

You should take a little time each day to observe your thoughts. I often find that I am thinking about a situation that later in the day comes into being, or I imagine that someone I know is upset, only to find out later that indeed they are upset. It never ceases to amaze me how many times, in my own daydreams and imaginings, I actually tune into very valid realities. It is true though, that until I began to accept the possibility that I indeed had psychic abilities, these thoughts and the events they were connected to escaped my notice.

In my classes I conducted an experiment that Jane Roberts used in her ESP classes. Each week, after class ended, I would tape a picture of something on the back of the door of the bathroom that class members used. During the week class members would work with these suggestions and then mentally try to envision what the image on the door was. The week that Clarence Dougherty came to class with a picture of a valentine heart and I took a drawing of a bright red heart off the back of the door, we called it a hit! Although it may sound silly, this type of experiment helps you to grow in confidence about your psychic abilities. As your confidence grows, your beliefs become stronger and therefore your abilities increase as well.

The real value in developing these abilities is that, when needed, they can be relied upon for answering far more important questions than what sits on the back of a door. You can learn to follow your intuitions in situations where you need to make choices and are not certain which way to turn. These can be important questions that affect your physical and mental well-being.

The other psychic sciences—astrology, numerology, tarot, or runes—involve more study. Some of you may feel inclined to undertake such study. If your life is way too busy for you to consider such an undertaking, you can seek the advice and knowledge of those who have studied these sciences.

A personalized astrological chart provides an excellent outline of your strengths and weaknesses. If prepared by a well-informed sincere astrologer, these charts can help us understand ourselves more deeply and choose directions.

Tarot readings—again, if done by a sincere and knowledgeable reader—can be enlightening, to say the least. I recently had my astrological chart done by Sheovaun T. La Londe. Sheovaun is a lovely young woman who, along with being a clairvoyant, has a deep and thorough understanding of the psychic sciences. In her readings she employs clairvoyance, astrology, numerology, the tarot, and runes. After our meeting, my feelings about my life and my work were confirmed. Because I am already quite aware of my own thoughts and beliefs I was not surprised by anything in the reading. I was, however, pleased at the accuracy of the reading. I received a very pertinent message through the use of rune stones, a psychic science that was new to me. The reading provided me with useful insights into my life. Because I am impressed with Sheovaun's knowledge and sincere desire to help her clients become more self-aware, I have asked her to do an interview for this book. The following material is taken from an interview with Sheovaun T. La Londe.

Sheri: Can you tell me a little bit about your background in the occult sciences?

Sheovaun: My interest in the occult began as a young child. I have been a student of the occult and metaphysics for the past twelve years. I have lived and studied in Europe, the Middle East, Central America, and North and West Africa. In those particular places I had the good fortune of meeting very fine teachers who have guided me along the path.

Sheri: In your work with others, how many different occult sciences do you employ?

Sheovaun: In my work with a client, I combine astrology, tarot, and either the numbers or the rune stones. It depends upon what I feel is most appropriate for that person, given what they are going through at that point.

Sheri: Would you explain to me a little bit about each of these sciences. How and why do they work?

Sheovaun: Astrology is a symbolic language describing basic human energies and their characteristics. At one's particular hour and place of birth the planets are in certain positions in the heavens which, during the course of one's life, help to measure the individual's strengths and weaknesses, assets and liabilities so that one can build a happy and constructive life. The horoscope shows *tendencies* in a person—not exactly what she or he will be. Usually there are major themes seen in the analysis of a chart.

Sheri: So in essence you are saying that the way the planets line up on the day of someone's birth influences and affects their characteristics and nature.

Sheovaun: Exactly. I'd like to point out that we have the power ultimately to rule our planetary structure. Although the chart shows potential, it does not lay claim as to *what* the person will do with that potential as she or he goes through life. That is entirely up to the individual.

Sheri: In other words one's horoscope is something like a blueprint.

Sheovaun: Exactly. The horoscope is a blueprint. It's a great help, I think, for some people who have difficulty understanding certain aspects of their nature. They can be born, for example, into a family in which their chart differs from their parents' and siblings'. They need, therefore, to recognize that their rhythms will be different from their family and immediate environment, thus perhaps their needs. As a result this may help the individual or client to feel less isolated, less misunderstood. It's also a real help to me in understanding the best possible approach to take with a client given their unique structure. For example, I would approach the session quite differently with an extroverted type than I would with an introvert.

Sheri: Could you explain to me a little bit about the tarot and also why our touch upon the cards helps influence the reading?

Sheovaun: Some clients who are new at this will come and I'll spread the cards out for them to pick those they are drawn to and they say, "Well, I can pick up any card, this doesn't make sense." I explain to them that it's their higher self guiding them to that particular card, so there is no accident that they chose the card they do. The tarot has long been regarded as one of the finest explanatory records of the supreme mysteries, one of the oldest bodies of wisdom known to us. Tradition has it that it was formulated vast eons ago by initiates who wished to make their cosmic wisdom available to those ready, ripe, and willing to pay the price in persistent study, time, effort, and attention. It's a book disguised as a pack of cards containing the accumulated occult and spiritual wisdom of the ages. The tarot can be considered the science of conscious integration. It's one of the many tools that throw light on the basic functions of ourselves, our daily life, the universe, and our work here.

Sheri: Exactly how do you work with them?

Sheovaun: I give the client the cards. I ask them to shuffle because that gives them an opportunity to put their vibrations into the cards. I want them to shuffle thoroughly. Then I have them cut the cards into three piles with the left hand. The left hand is used because it is considered the receptive side of a person. They cut into three piles, shuffle each separately, make one pile out of that, and then we go into various spreads.

Sheri: By spreads you mean different patterns in which you lay out the cards?

Sheovaun: Right. I start with the horseshoe spread. There's also the Celtic cross, a horoscope spread, and a southern cross. It's all a matter of time as to which ones we focus on. The first spread gives me a clue as to the client's state of mind early in the reading. A lot of them are nervous and that usually shows up. As the hour progresses, however, they become more comfortable and then we usually get much more information because they are becoming receptive.

Sheri: Now I would imagine that you have studied the cards, so that when you look at a card you know what it represents.

Sheovaun: Yes. Each card on its own, with its various symbols, is chock full of information. However, the cards will change according to the other cards that are laid with them. Each card means something, but then I'll draw two more cards on that particular card and the meaning will either give us more information, or it changes the structure of the information. Also with each spread, each card is in a position that is pertinent to some experience in the person's life—past, present, future—or in position of relationship, health, sex, things like that. So each card takes on a different color or different theme according to both its position and the cards that fall with it.

Sheri: So the cards each have meanings. The clients, through their own vibrations, impact on what cards show up. If the reader is intuitive, and has a knowledge of the cards and the way that the patterns lay out, he or she can extrapolate information for the client.

Sheovaun: Exactly. I do not know how someone could do readings if they weren't clairvoyant. In my experience I find that it is necessary to tune in to something higher, to be receptive. Sometimes I'll hear voices in the readings, sometimes I'll see colors, but I have to get my critical mind out of the way so that the information pertinent to the reading can come forth freely. For example, if information comes through and my critical mind says, "Yes, but how do you know that, Sheovaun?" then I am allowing myself to get in the way. Of course it's important to be discriminating with what comes through, and to be careful how you phrase things to people. To give you an example, I had a pregnant woman come to see me years ago. I was concerned about the child, whether she would be able to carry the child full term. Rather than say, "You may have complications, and at worst lose the child," I advised her to be sure to get a lot of rest and cut back her activities toward the latter part of her term. As it turns out, it was touch and go there, but because she heeded the advice she was out of danger. It's important not to instill fear and dread into a client—that's a destructive seed to plant. I always try to leave each client with a ray of hope. I do believe that if you've had a reading and feel miserable or upset or gloomy, then it hasn't been a constructive reading on the part of the clairvoyant.

Sheri: Should we move on to numbers? I was amazed at the accuracy of the numbers in the readings that you did with me.

Sheovaun: Yes. Like the tarot, numbers don't lie. There's a vibration to each number and letter. All numbers are reduced to a single digit except what we call master numbers and that's an eleven, a twenty-two, and a thirty-three. Thirty-three is rare, not a lot of numerologists I know of use that in their work.

Sheri: How many numbers are utilized? From one to what?

Sheovaun: One to ten, but ten is reduced again to one, so it's really one to nine. In numerology the belief is held that we experience nine-year chapters. For example each year carries its own universal vibration (1987 = 7) as well as the individual's personal vibration for that year. You might be in a one-personal year, which would mean new beginnings, new activities opening up, a new nine-year chapter opening up for you. Or you might be coming to a close of your nine-year cycle and be in a nine-personal vibration, indicating this is a year in which to tie up loose ends, take care of unfinished business. There is also the yin or yang, the positive or negative, to each number and the vibration it carries. Numerology is also as old as recorded history and it's the simple science of vibration. This applies to you and your personal relation to the world. Numerology aids us in discovering where our energies would best be directed. It gives us deeper insight into character and personality, as well as our personal vibration for any day, month, or year. This is all derived from the breakdown or analysis of your name at birth and your birthdate. You will always have the same birthdate—that you cannot change—so the challenge number, the destiny birth-path number, remains for life. People do change their names, but by doing so they change their vibrations. A name may bring very difficult lessons; however, I think it's important that you understand that your higher self chose the structure of your birth plan for a very special reason and that by working on any difficulties that may come up as a result, you could be given the chance to clear away old karma.

Sheri: Let me see if I can sum this up. We've got basically one to nine numbers that we work with. The numbers represent different aspects of life and ourselves. Based on the way the number of letters in our name and the day, month, and year in our birth date add up, a birth and name pattern are determined.

Sheovaun: That's right. Through that you discover the story of a person's life—what the soul has come to learn and express. You see a story, as in astrology. It's a different science, another way of doing it. There's a pattern that becomes apparent. What people should know is that I may see a particularly tough year ahead. To be aware of it, to be forewarned, is to be forearmed. They don't have to dive into the despair or the negative side of that number. They can use the lessons that that number can also give. For example, a nine, as said earlier, is endings. It is, to be sure, a difficult time in one's life. It represents finishing up, creating a conclusion, summing up the past nine years. There are losses involved. There's responsibility. But it's also a great time for publishing, for writing, for long-distance travel. Therefore I try and coach people to see the brighter side, without being blinded, of course, to the darker side.

Sheri: Now the rune stones? Can you tell me a little about them? Who were they created by?

Sheovaun: They were created by the Druids, the Celtics. It's an ancient alphabetical script, a means of communication with the knowledge of our subconscious minds. The runes are considered an oracle that reveals one's hidden fears, motivations, and inner strength. They're very similar to the *I Ching*. It's just another tool. With the *I Ching* you can throw coins or matchsticks or whatever. With the runes you either throw these stones or you place your hand into a bag containing the stones. Your higher self guides you in selecting the particular stone which carries the most pertinent message for you.

Sheri: So on the stone there is a symbol that represents a particular message?

Sheovaun: Yes. I have my clients put their hand into a bag containing the stones. I ask them to meditate. This can be a very private experience; there is no need for them to tell me what their question is about. Moreover, this is not a yes or no question. They will not get that kind of response. It's more like, "Grant me more information on a particular subject." I have them meditate on that thought before they draw the stone out, to give it some real conscious thought. Then when they feel ready, they'll feel the appropriate stone either get stuck between their fingers or they just can't let go of it. Somehow they'll know that that's the appropriate stone to pick out. Then I interpret for them what the message for that particular symbol represents.

Sheri: Do your clients usually find the message on the stones pertinent?

Sheovaun: I'd say eighty percent of them are blown away by the accuracy. But I'll get some people who have more difficulty relating to the message. After all, it can be a bit abstract or too poetic for some.

Sheri: What is it that is most important to you to achieve in your work?

Sheovaun: When people come to me, they are putting a tremendous amount of trust in me. They would like me to come up with answers or solutions for them and it is a tremendous responsibility. I'm aware of that. I want to give them information on themselves. I try to avoid fortune-telling, that's just too easy. I want them to understand that ultimately it's their responsibility to take control of their lives. I try to give them a ray of hope and light into a situation that may look bleak for them, to encourage them to tap into their unconscious, into their higher self.

The cards, the numbers, the runes are all catalysts for them to reach their hidden side and see the potential. With the guidance of the cards, the numbers, runes, and natal horoscope, I try to make it clear that it is probably their attitude to the situation that needs altering. I find that concerning romance people may come with broken hearts and want to look at the relationship to discover the why's and how's of what's going on. The more difficult the situation, usually the more profound the lessons involved. I will try to encourage them to register what's happening to themselves, and around them, rather than reacting to it all; to be as objective as possible within an obviously subjective or painful situation. Otherwise the vision becomes clouded, emotions stir up, and one acts with blind force rather than reason.

I know this may sound easy to say and I understand how difficult it can be, but this earth plane is a testing field and we are here to grow as conscious beings so that we may improve our lot and the lives of those we share this "field" with. In my practice I ask for divine guidance so that the information brought forth be of the highest good of my client and of all. I guess what I would like is for people to awaken to the idea of being responsible for their life and to gain understanding of their experiences through observation and cognitive perception. In this world it is so easy to be run by our subconscious, to become like machines. Through the various divine sciences, the higher self can be contacted and peace restored.

Sheri: Are you available to do readings for people?

Sheovaun: Yes, my clients are from all walks of life, and I'm very available. I usually ask my clients to think about why they are coming, just what it is they are seeking through a session with me. In this way they can begin to think about some of their questions beforehand.

I'm sure you can all see how fascinating the occult sciences are. If used as a tool, these sciences can be enormously useful to us. If you realize that ultimately the power, the energy, and the responsibility are your own, then these tools can be used to help you purposefully direct your energy. Anything that helps you gain deeper understanding and perspective on your life is worthwhile. Therefore, feel free to engage in the study and use of these sciences. Remember always that you have the power to create change. Neither the stars, numbers, cards, nor runes control you, and yet through your work with them you can gain a clearer picture of how you have been creating your life.

Appendix H
Channeling

Channeling is an ancient art of communication. It provides a means for beings not physically focused on the earth to communicate with beings who are. In simpler terms it allows for communication to take place between the spirit world and the physical one.

There are many forces around us that we do not perceive. Energy exists that we do not see, and sounds exist that we do not hear. The physical plane exists on a different vibrational frequency from the spirit world. The spirit world vibrates at a faster rate, as it is not composed of physical matter. In order for communication to take place between the two worlds, a receptive channel must exist—thus the channel or medium.

In most forms of mediumship, the channel enters into a trance state. At this time the communicating entity takes over the body of the channel. This process is agreed upon and not forced! The channel and the communicating entity are working together.

In my experience, the communicating entities have always been caring, concerned individuals who display genuine love and affection toward the people they are interacting with. Whatever fear I may have had regarding talking to a "spook" has changed into admiration for my new friends and gratitude to the channels for allowing this process to take place.

I find it very fascinating that many people on the earth today are developing the art of channeling. More people are willing to accept what they do not physically see. At the same time, the communicating entities keep urging us to open up spiritually and perceive how we are forming our present experience and our world. We are being called upon to take responsibility for our thoughts and our actions.

I was very fortunate to take part in Jane Roberts's ESP classes in which Seth spoke freely and honestly. The experience of communicating with a nonphysical being is enlightening and profoundly moving. It is also reassuring to sense the vitality that exists after physical life.

There is much that we can learn from our friends on the other side. Because they are nonphysical, they naturally possess a broad viewpoint on physical matters. I know that this was true of Seth and of the many nonphysical friends and teachers I have been acquainted with.

I am very pleased that my dear friend Richard Wolinsky has agreed to an interview for this chapter. Rich, who has a master's degree in philosophy, attended the Seth classes for many years. He is now channeling himself. Martenard, the entity who speaks through Rich, is knowledgeable, kind, and caring. The following information is taken from an interview with Rich and his channel personality Martenard.

Sheri: Can you tell me a little bit about your professional life outside of channeling work?

Rich: For the past decade I've been the editor of the program guide magazine for KPFA FM, a noncommercial, listener-sponsored radio station in Berkeley, California. I also cohost a radio program of interviews and reviews in genre fiction—mostly mysteries and science fiction. I have been involved in that for ten years as well.

Sheri: How long have you been interested in psychic phenomena?

Rich: For a long time. I would say that there has been an underlying interest that goes back as far as high school. When I was approximately fifteen years old, I began reading science fiction. A book entitled *The Stars, My Destination* really caught my attention. It was about traveling beyond your body. At about the same time I read a book entitled *Slan*, a science-fiction novel about people with mental powers. These were the first science-fiction books that I read, and they were all about psychic phenomena. You could say that I was kind of hooked! In college I was obsessed with Atlantis. At the time I was also involved with studies in gnostisism, as were many of my friends. I found that in graduate school the entire concept of the transcendent took a backseat to the study of language. I began moving away from that in my own head sometime before I actually started reading the Seth books. When the Seth books came along, it was as if a whole new world had opened up to me. Six months later I began attending Jane Roberts's ESP classes.

Sheri: How long did you take part in the ESP classes?

Rich: I first attended in March of 1973. The first time that Seth came through I jumped two feet in the air! I began attending regularly in the end of May 1973. Except for a couple of vacation breaks I went practically every week from then until Jane ended the regular classes in the end of February 1975. In Sue Watkin's books, *Conversations with Seth* I am referred to as Will Petrosky, for those interested.

Sheri: Would you say that you were really impressed with the Seth classes?

Rich: They blew me away! They changed my life!

Sheri: Did you ever think, at that time, that you would get involved in channeling yourself?

Rich: No. I figured that I would never be able to give up that little space of myself to allow someone to speak through me. I thought it was not in the cards. However, after I moved to California, my two roommates and I played with a Ouija board one night. When asked what I would be doing for a living, it kept going to the medium on the board and spelling out that this event would occur when I was thirty-six. In fact, I started channeling when I was thirty-four. It wasn't until I was thirty-six, however, that it actually seemed viable as a primary or secondary career.

Sheri: How did it happen for you that you started channeling—did it happen all at once, or was there a gradual development?

Rich: About three years earlier a friend of mine by the name of Richard Lavin began to channel. I was one of the people responsible for helping to guide him through the entire process. In February 1985 I had bought a house, but due to various reasons I was unable to move in for a few months. I was still living in a cramped one-bedroom apartment. One evening I felt depressed about the fact that I had to remain in this apartment for another month and a half. I'm not certain why, but something clicked in me. I had taken self-hypnosis classes about three years earlier. I knew how to enter a deep hypnotic trance. So I lay down on my couch, closed my eyes, and using hypnotic cueing entered into a trance state. I then said, "Okay, if there's anybody there—speak up!"

I got basically almost gibberish, you could say. I don't know if this can go in print but it was something like "puh puh puh." At that point I assumed, "Well, that's as good as it gets. That's it! Good-bye, it's been nice knowing you." However, when I called up Richard Lavin in San Diego and told him, he said, "Wow, now you can channel!" I thought that it didn't seem too likely; however, Richard asked me not to worry. He said that he was coming up the following week and that we would try it together. I figured that it was worth another try.

Richard came to my house about a week later, sat me down, and I went into trance again. This time when I got the "puh puh puh," he told me to allow the words to form in my consciousness and then to speak them. In other words, I would consciously be taking an active role in the process rather than assuming that my mouth was going to move without me doing anything. And so I tried it. Not only did the words come out, but they came out in an accent. It took about three sessions before I finally got deep enough to ask Martenard his name and he told me. I would have preferred something a little bit shorter and snappier.

Sheri: How did the Martenard sessions develop to the point where you were getting more information?

Rich: The difference between the earlier sessions and the ones that followed was simply a matter of me being able to put myself as far away as possible to allow more information through. The entire development of the channeling process after that, and this is good advice for anyone who desires to channel, is a question of practice, practice, practice. You need to be willing to allow information through which could be "proven wrong," and then to keep practicing to improve the quality of the material. In other words, essentially it involves the same hard work that it would take to develop any kind of skill or art. That's where the difficulty comes in. Anybody can channel first time out, but it's the exercise and practice that improves one's work. At least this seems to be true for the conscious channels. For those who seem to leave their bodies fully unconscious, it appears that the material comes through far more advanced the first time out. Some are totally unconscious channels, and have been from the word one.

Sheri: By that you mean that they are not conscious of what is taking place?

Rich: I mean that when they go into trance, they claim to completely leave their bodies. They have no memory when it's occurring. There's no "development" of the process. As soon as they let the personality in, it appears that the personality is full-blown and all the information is full-blown.

Sheri: In your case, then, you were more conscious of the process and it therefore took more effort to allow yourself to go deeper and really let this process happen.

Rich: You got it.

Sheri: What are your hopes for your channeling work? What would you like to see develop?

Rich: At this point my aim is still to be as good as I can be and to make the channeling as good as the channeling can be. I look upon channeling as an ongoing, never completed process. Part of it has to do with the fact that the primary person involved in the channeling is the person doing the channeling. If the channeling can't help or change or make that person grow, then you have to examine their whole process. So in that regard, I would hope that as the channeling continues, I'll continue to grow as a person. Beyond that, Martenard has his own agenda, which is simply to get his word out. He is willing to go through whatever route I need to take. I'm not a publicity hound, nor am I interested in trying to set myself up on some kind of exalted level—not that I think I could get away with it if I did, but I can not imagine myself doing that. I have some small groups and right now I have been doing a number of remote individual readings, which I enjoy more than readings where the person is present, oddly enough. That seems to be where my work lies now. For the past nine months, in an on-and-off basis, Martenard has been dictating a book, working in a collaboration with a friend of mine. This is also an ongoing process.

Sheri: From my time with you and Martenard, and knowing you as a close friend, I can say that you have certainly grown as a result of the Martenard development. The Martenard information has developed as well, so you have every reason to be pleased with the work. I was hoping that you would be willing to allow Martenard to come through and impart a brief message to my readers.

Rich: I would be glad to. One moment.

Sheri: Hello, Martenard! Thank you so much for your presence here today. It has been some time since I have spoken with you.

Martenard: Indeed!

Sheri: How are you doing?

Martenard: We are at the present time entering this physical body and noticing the air, and the sense of smell, and the sense of hearing that is occurring at this time. It is an interesting phenomenon for those who are not, in your terms, in physical reality.

Sheri: I would imagine so. How is the weather out there in California—pleasant for you?

Martenard: It is always pleasant, my friend. Understand that the weather is part of the natural cycles of the earth and is, indeed, the earth's greatest self-correcting mechanism. And every time you see a wild thunderstorm, it is the earth cleaning itself, scouring itself and creating itself anew.

Sheri: I do understand and thank you. I was hoping to ask you a question or two that I believe my readers will be interested in. First, I was wondering if there is a reason why you choose to speak?

Martenard: Now indeed. Understand that myself and my colleagues have chosen to enter these bodies because your race has requested, so to speak, alternative information— alternative viewpoints—to aid you in getting you over the hump, and that hump, of course, concerns the great transformations of consciousness that are occurring on your planet at this time. The so-called millennial changes, if you will. Now there are a number of "energies" who have chosen to enter temporarily at least, your physical world. Now, in your terms, these entities have been "dead" or never born, but all of them have been with you and your race all the way, in your terms. We are, so to speak, your spirit guides, your companions, your friends, and oftentimes in physical reality, your colleagues. Now we choose to help you here, for indeed you have requested it. As Seth once stated, we are as bottles sent back from your future selves to your current selves—bottles containing information about who you are and in your terms, who you will be.

Sheri: So you speak in answer to our request and also out of a desire to help us make needed changes.

Martenard: Indeed! This is why we have come. Now you, of course, do as you wish. And understand that we are not infallible gods but merely, though not so merely, individuals, a portion of God certainly, but individuals and groups who are here to give you more information and different sorts of information than you, in your conscious state, are not normally, in your terms, privy to. Now I say we are not infallible gods, but to a certain degree we and you are infallible gods. But we are not to be worshiped and our word is not to be taken as gospel.

Sheri: Right. When you say we are in part infallible gods you mean that we are all a part of God.

Martenard: Indeed! And we are all, we—meaning ourselves and yourselves—are all the gods, and to that degree all gods are perfect and infallible.

Sheri: And to that degree all gods are imperfect—Yes?

Martenard: It depends, my friend, upon what you call perfect and imperfect.

Sheri: I mean possessing the ability to make a mistake.

Martenard: My friend, there are no mistakes. There are only decisions and choices. And all choices are made for a purpose, for a reason.

Sheri: So in essence, even if something appears as a mistake, if you are learning from it . . .

Martenard: You are always learning from it. Therefore it is never a mistake. And oftentimes what appears to be a mistake in the short run, of course, sets up energy that creates different realities later on. Sometimes for example a small war can avert a nuclear one—a divorce can avert a suicide—a trauma can avert a catastrophe.

Sheri: Yes, I see what you mean. It's very interesting. Do you have a particular message for the readers of my book?

Martenard: The message is simply the one that we have been saying over and over. That you are the gods that you think you need to worship. That you are the gods that you are afraid to acknowledge. That you are indeed the gods who create this world and all the worlds. That you are indeed the gods of your own lives. That gods work in their own mysterious ways and you work in your own mysterious ways. And it is part of your great joy and creativity that as those mysterious ways become manifest, they become miracles. You are, my friends, all that you wish to be and you always have been. You create your world through your beliefs, your ideas, your hopes, your dreams, your fears, and your expectations. As you grow and achieve new spiritual understanding, you will gain consciously a greater control over those realities you have created and you are doing it now! This process is ongoing; it is also, my friends, accelerating. And as you grow and change and fully accept your godhood, so indeed your godhood will fully accept you. If there is any message we can give, it is to live your lives honestly, graciously, and in love. And by living your lives honestly, graciously, and with love toward yourself and toward others, you indeed create a greater and more spiritual world for yourselves. This is our message.

Sheri: It is a very beautiful message and I thank you very much. It is my honor to bring this material into the world through my book, and I feel that my readers will deeply appreciate it also. I thank you for your presence today, your presence always, my friend, Martenard.

Martenard: And we thank you for yours!

(For further information about Richard Wolinsky, see references.)

References

Dr. Robert Atkins
  400 East 56th Street
  New York, NY

Austin Seth Center
  The purpose is to enhance human dignity everywhere by
  teaching a philosophy that empowers people to achieve
  positive life changes with love, fun, and awareness.
  Publisher quarterly magazine—*Reality Change*
  P.O. Box 7786
  Austin, TX 78713–7786
  (512) 479–8909

Carolyn Bengston
  Certified Acupuncturist and Massage Therapist
  New York, NY

Edward Berk, Holistic Herbologist
  247 West 11th Street
  New York, NY 10014
  (212) 691–0514

Boericke and Tafel
  Providing high-quality homeopathic medicines, literature,
  and services. Boericke and Tafel began its career in 1835.
  Concerned with "accuracy, honesty and fair dealing."
  1011 Arch Street
  Philadelphia, PA 19107
  (215) 922–2967

Boiron-Borneman, Inc.
Established in 1932, the company mission is to give home-opathy its rightful place in the United States by providing the community with the highest quality homeopathic medi-cines and services. They are particularly concentrating their efforts in:
1. Financing rigorous scientific projects in fundamental and clinical research through the Boiron Research Foun-dation, created in 1982 in the United States.
2. Supporting a wide program of education in homeopa-thy through the Boiron Institute, created in 1985 in the United States.
Medicines and Literature
1208 Amosland Road
Norwood, PA 19074
(215) 532–2035

Center of the Light
Eva and Eugene Graf, Directors
P. O. Box 540
Great Barrington, MA
(413) 229–2396
"The Center of the Light is the educational and retreat facility of the Church of Christ Consciousness. The church is a healing church moving in the divinity of the entire human family, and the potential of every individual to experience a real and personal relationship with God. The church's paramount goal is to nourish, teach, and offer spiritual support to the human family and the earth. The church is nondenomenational and recognizes many approaches to physical, mental, and spiritual growth and well-being."

Center of the Light
Linda Burnam, Healer, Teacher
Specialized course of study in facial rejuvenation
Graf Body Systems class, the Angelic Kingdom, and Crystals
P. O. Box 540
Great Barrington, MA
(413) 229–2705

Crystal Council, Inc.
Anne Hatfield President
"Crystal Council, Inc. owns a crystal mine in Arkansas and is dedicated to mining with respect for the land, earth stewardship, planetary healing, and ethical business practices. Everyone in the company, from miners to managers, from shippers to shareholders, love the crystals for their healing properties. You can be assured that the beautiful healing crystals you buy from this mine have been exposed to nothing but love and respect from the moment they emerge from the earth."

Write for a free catalogue (specify retail or wholesale):
Crystal Council, Inc.
Dept. SP
4456 Bodega Avenue
Petaluma, CA 94952
(707) 763–3598

Crystal Gardens—Joyce Kaessinger and Constance Barrett
Seminars, meditations, crystals and literature
"We believe that crystals are here to help empower us to create personal and world realities which are filled with love and light. In our shop we assist customers in selecting crystals appropriate for them from our unique collection of gems, minerals, and jewelry. As a resource and educational center, we publish a monthly newsletter and offer seminars on crystals and related subjects."
Crystal Gardens
c/o The Soho Emporium
375 West Broadway, New York, NY 10012
(212) 431–6439

Foundation for the Advancement of World Peace
Elaine Seiler, Director
Box 799
Great Barrington, MA
The focus of this foundation is peace education, personal empowerment, and worldwide giving of quartz crystal as a symbol of peace.

Luke Gatto, Teacher
  Networking Homeopathic Practitioners
  P. O. Box 9278
  Sante Fe, NM 87504

Dr. Irwin Gelernt, Surgeon
  25 East 69th Street
  New York, NY 10021
  (212) 517–8600

Harry Edwards Spiritual Healing Sanctuary
  Mr. and Mrs. Ray Branch, Spiritual Healers
  Burrows Lea
  Shere Guildford
  Surrey GU5 9QG
  England
  Phone: 011 44 48641 2054
  "The Harry Edwards Spiritual Healing Sanctuary was
  founded by Harry Edwards in 1946 with the express purpose of helping sick and suffering people, both in the
  United Kingdom and all over the world, through spiritual
  healing. During the forty-plus years the Sanctuary has
  been in existence, countless thousands of people have
  been helped, the great majority of them suffering from a
  variety of ill conditions for which the doctors have been
  unable to do any more. It is a tribute to the success,
  mainly to the absent healing directive, that so many have
  been able to report improvement, if not a full overcoming
  of their troubles. Although Harry Edwards passed on in
  1976, the work of the Sanctuary has been maintained in
  the Harry Edwards tradition by Ray and Joan Branch,
  who were his close associates in the work at Shere for
  fourteen years. In all the years of the Sanctuary's existence, no charge has ever been made to any patient for
  healing help given, and the Sanctuary has therefore been
  supported entirely by free-will donations."

When writing, be sure to include your name, age, address, and a brief description of your problem. You can
mention the medical diagnosis if any, and indicate what
symptoms stand out in your mind as the most disturbing.

Institute for the Advancement of Health
The Institute for the Advancement of Health is the national voluntary organization for mind-body health. As such, they explore connections between the mind and physical health. Through its publications (a quarterly journal, *Advances*, and their newsletter, *The Mind Body Health Digest*) and projects they report developments in this fast growing field.
16 East 53rd Street
Dept. S.P.
New York, NY 10022
(212) 832–8282

Sheovaun T. La Londe
Clairvoyant specializing in tarot, astrology, and numerology
New York, NY
(212) 860–4772

Richard Lavin, Channel for "Ecton." Intuitive Counselor
In addition to making frequent trips to the West Coast, Richard is also available for long-distance channelings.
P.O. Box 691
Waimanalo, HI 96795
(808) 259-8115

Joyce Liechenstein
Counselor, psychotherapist, Neuro-Linguistic Programming practitioner of hypnosis, Reiki therapist, MariEl Healer Individual, couple and group counseling—meditation and creative visualization classes.
New York, NY 10009
(212) 673–4427

Joan Magner
Psychic, Tarot reader
P.O. Box 1312
Torrance, CA 90505-01312

Dr. Barry Mankowitz, Surgeon
Marathon, Florida

Nancy Migdol—Healer—M.S.W.
Offering emotional and spiritual support and guidance in areas involving individual growth and self love, deeper commitment within relationships, and all parenting and

family issues. Confidential, professional support provided with care.
Sarasota Fla.
(813) 349-1830

Monroe Institute
Internationally known for its work in the effects of sound-wave forms on human behavior. The resulting technology, called Hemi-Sync, has led to breakthroughs in the areas of consciousness exploration, stress and anxiety reduction, pain control, accelerated learning, sleep restoration, peak performance, enhanced creativity, therapy, and medicine.
Route 1, Box 175
Faber, VA 22938–9749
(804) 361–1252

National Federation of Spiritual Healers
Available to help you locate healers
(Please include a self-addressed envelope with requests.)
Old Manor Farm Studio
Church Street
Sunbury-on-Thames
Middlesex TW16 6RG
England
Phone: Sunbury (0932) 783164/5

New York Open Center
A center for the exploration of the humanities and the arts from a holistic perspective
83 Spring Street
New York, NY 10012
(212) 219–2527

Carole A. Nostrand, Food and Diet Consultant
131 West 11th Street
New York, NY 10014
(212) 691–9384

Sheri Perl, Teacher, Healer
Private consultations and seminars in Healing and the Seth Material
Working with emotional as well as physical difficulties
P.O. Box 1007
New York, NY 10014

Dr. Daniel Present, Gastroenterologist
 12 East 86th Street
 New York, NY 10028
 (212) 861–2000

Dr. Martin L. Rossman
 Working with imagery techniques
 Collaborative Medicine Center
 Mill Valley, CA

School for Creative Movement
 Jack Weiner, Director
 Classes and workshops integrating movement and dance
 with healing
 20 West 20th Street
 New York, NY 10011
 (212) 929–0929

Rick Stack, classes in the Seth Material and Metaphysics
 New York, NY
 (212) 580–3185

UCLA Pain Management Center
 Department of Anesthesiology
 UCLA School of Medicine
 Center for the Health Sciences, AR-200
 Los Angeles, CA 90024
 (213) 825–4291
 The UCLA Pain Management Center provides education
 and treatment of patients with acute and chronic pain.
 Their staff includes specialists from the areas of neurol-
 ogy, psychology, psychiatry, physical therapy, acupunc-
 ture, anesthesiology, dentistry, and internal medicine.

Richard Wolinsky, Channel-Intuitive Counselor
 Available for individual, group, and remote channeling.
 P.O. Box 1173
 El Cerrito, CA 94530
 (415) 525-5344

Suggested Reading

Atkins, Robert. *Dr. Atkins' Nutrition Breakthrough*. New York: Bantam, 1982.

Bach, Edward. *The Bach Flower Remedies*. New Canaan, Conn: Keats, 1952.

Benson, Herbert. *The Relaxation Response*. New York: Avon, 1976.

Bristol, Claude M. and Sherman, Harold. *TNT: The Power Within You*. Englewood Cliffs, N.J: Prentice-Hall, 1954.

Bry, Adelaide. *Visualization: Directing the Movies of Your Mind*. New York: Barnes and Noble, 1978.

Cousin, Norman. *Anatomy of an Illness*. New York: Avon, 1979.

Cousins, Norman. *The Healing Heart*. New York: Avon, 1983.

Edwards, Harry. *The Healing Intelligence*. London: Healer, 1965.

Gawain, Shakti. *Creative Visualization*. Mill Valley, Cal.: Whatever, 1978.

Geer, Richard H. *Star + Gate*. Orinda, Cal.: Cloud Enterprises, 1984.

Hay, Louise L. *You Can Heal Your Life*. Santa Monica, Cal. Hay House, 1984.

Keyes, Ken. *The Handbook to Higher Consciousness*. Coos Bay, Ore. Living Love, 1975.

MacLaine, Shirley. *Out on a Limb*. New York: Bantam, 1988.

Mitchell, Ellinor R. *Plain Talk about Acupuncture*. New York: Whalehall, 1987.

Nostrand, Carole A. *A Handbook for Improving Your Diet.* New York: Eatongude Press, 1985.

Raphaell, Katrina. *Crystal Enlightenment.* New York: Aurora Press, 1985.

Roberts, Jane. *The Nature of Personal Reality.* Englewood Cliffs, N.J.: Prentice-Hall, 1974.

Roberts, Jane. *The Seth Material.* Englewood Cliffs, N.J.: Prentice-Hall, 1970.

Roberts, Jane. *Seth Speaks.* Englewood Cliffs, N.J.: Prentice-Hall, 1972.

Rossman, Martin L. *Healing Yourself.* New York: Walker, 1987.

Seiler, Elaine and Lantieri, Linda. *Quartz Crystal: A Gift from the Earth.* Great Barrington, Mass.: Resourse Management, 1985.

Siegel, Bernie S. *Love Medicine and Miracles.* New York: Harper & Row, 1988.

Simonton, Carl O. and Mathews-Simonton, Stephanie. *Getting Well Again.* Los Angeles: Tharcher, 1987.

Smith, Trevor. *Homeopathic Medicine.* Wellingborough, Eng.: Thorsons, 1982.

Walker, Dale. *The Crystal Book.* Sunol, Cal. Crystal, 1983.

Watkins, Susan M. *Conversations with Seth,* vols. 1 and 2. Englewood Cliffs, N.J.: Prentice-Hall, 1980, 1981.

"French cookery skillfully adapted for healthful eating . . ."
—Nathan Pritikin

Deliciously Low

THE GOURMET GUIDE TO LOW-SODIUM, LOW-FAT, LOW-CHOLESTEROL, LOW-SUGAR COOKING

by
Harriet Roth

Former director, Pritikin Longevity Center Cooking School

Delight your tastebuds while protecting your health—with this unique collection of spectacular "alternative" recipes from a noted pioneer in low-risk, high-quality cooking.

- More than 300 creative and exciting recipes
- Complete nutritional information, including per-serving content of 20 essential nutrients for each dish
- Sample menus, technique lessons, and hints for garnishing, serving, and storing, and much more

"An excellent choice for the gourmet cook who decides it's time to cut down on sodium, fat, cholesterol and sugar."
—Dr. Jean Mayer, *Los Angeles Times*

Helpful suggestions and alternatives to sugar-laden desserts."
—*Bon Appétit*

There's an epidemic with 27 million victims. And no visible symptoms.

It's an epidemic of people who can't read.

Believe it or not, 27 million Americans are functionally illiterate, about one adult in five.

The solution to this problem is you... when you join the fight against illiteracy. So call the Coalition for Literacy at toll-free **1-800-228-8813** and volunteer.

Volunteer Against Illiteracy. The only degree you need is a degree of caring.